PELICAN BOOKS

FRAMES OF MIND

Liam Hudson was born in 1933 and grew up in the
London suburb of Sutton. He was educated at Whit-
gift School and Exeter College, Oxford, where he
studied first modern history and then philosophy and
psychology. In 1957 he moved to the Psychological
Laboratory, Cambridge, and took his Ph.D. there
four years later. In 1965 he became a member of the
newly formed Research Centre at King's College,
Cambridge, and he was elected a Fellow of the College
in 1966, in which year his book *Contrary Imaginations*
was published (available in Pelicans). In 1968 he became Professor of Educational Sciences at the University of Edinburgh. Liam Hudson is married, with
three sons and a daughter. His interests are largely
domestic: painting, collecting porcelain, and privacy.

LIAM HUDSON

FRAMES OF MIND

Ability, Perception
and Self-perception in the
Arts and Sciences

PENGUIN BOOKS

Penguin Books Ltd, Harmondsworth, Middlesex, England
Penguin Books Inc., 7110 Ambassador Road, Baltimore, Maryland 21207, U.S.A.
Penguin Books Australia Ltd, Ringwood, Victoria, Australia

—

First published by Methuen 1968
Published in Pelican Books 1970
Copyright © Liam Hudson, 1968

—

Made and printed in Great Britain by
C. Nicholls & Company Ltd
Set in Monotype Plantin

To
BERNADINE

CONTENTS

ACKNOWLEDGEMENTS

THROUGHOUT the last three years, the period in which this book was prepared and written, I have enjoyed the financial support of the Nuffield Foundation, and have been housed in the Research Centre of King's College, Cambridge. I am indebted to the Director and Trustees of the Foundation, and to the Provost and Fellows of King's. I am grateful to Dr C. R. B. Joyce and Dr M. R. Parlett who have collaborated with me in certain of the experiments described here. And several people have been kind enough to comment on an earlier draft of the book: Dr K. W. Blyth, Dr E. R. Leach, Dr M. R. Parlett and Dr R. M. Young. Their criticisms and suggestions have been invaluable. None the less, the responsibility for the text is mine entirely. I am also grateful to members of staff at the schools where I tested; and to the undergraduates, schoolboys and schoolgirls who have given me the information on which this book is based.

1968   *King's College, Cambridge*

CHAPTER I

IN INTRODUCTION

LIKE its predecessor *Contrary Imaginations*, this book deals with differences in human intellect – differences, that is, in the ways in which people think, in the frames of mind they characteristically adopt. My first study, eleven years ago, concerned arts specialists and scientists; and this core of interest in the arts and sciences has remained. But the territory encompassed has widened, and is widening still. I now find myself dealing not only with the relation of intellectual development to personality, but also with the academic context in which such development takes place; not only with the reality of the individual's situation, but also his perception of it.

The work reported in *Contrary Imaginations* revolved around a distinction of type. Two kinds of clever schoolboy were distinguished: the converger and the diverger. These differed not only in the bias of their mental abilities, but also in their choice between the arts and sciences, in their interests and attitudes, and in their expression of emotion. The converger excelled in the conventional intelligence test; specialized in physical science or classics; held conventional attitudes; pursued technical, mechanical interests in his spare time; and was emotionally inhibited. The diverger, by contrast, excelled at open-ended tests (tests, that is, which do not have a single right answer); specialized in the arts or in biology; held unconventional attitudes; had interests which were connected in one way or another with people; and, emotionally speaking, was uninhibited. Such differences have implications both for the study of career choice and of originality; and much of the second half of *Contrary Imaginations* was taken up with discussion of these.

Having described the differences between converger and diverger, and drawn out both positive and negative implications, I seemed to occupy something of a bridgehead position. There were a number of directions in which I could explore. This book gives an account of those explorations; and also attempts a synthesis, fitting the various elements of my work into a coherent pattern.

Disregarding local forays, I have five lines of research to describe. First, in Chapters 2 and 3, some work at key points in the correlational groundwork of convergence and divergence: relating these qualities, for instance, to authoritarianism and masculinity. Although less than breathtaking, the results introduce ideas germane to much of what follows. Second, in Chapters 4 and 5, boys' perceptions of the arts and sciences. This is a track well-trodden; boys' prejudices and presuppositions are huge and often amusing. Earlier studies fail, however, to relate these to the behaviour of the individuals who profess them. Here, I think, this weakness is overcome; and evidence about such 'cultural stereotypes' now dovetails with the rest. They also have ramifications, especially in the field of language, that no one foresaw. Chapter 6 reports a third group of studies that I was led into almost coincidentally. At first I tried to relate boys' perceptions of themselves to certain external facts about them: their academic speciality, for example, and their success at school. Gradually the theme of self-perception gained momentum, and led on to a fourth set of experiments. These – described in Chapter 7 – were attempts to modify boys' divergent skills. Here, it seemed, their self-perception, their sense of what behaviour was appropriate, was limiting the amount of mental fluency they were willing to reveal. Finally, in Chapter 8, two pieces of work of a more practical kind: a study of an experimental method of teaching, and an experiment in university selection. These, again, bear on the book's recurring theme: the influence of the individual's perception, both of his academic context and of himself, on the intellectual ability he is free to display.

Before getting down to the results, there are two other points. Over the last three years I have grown less alarmed by theory, and have begun to edge out of the role of the 'simple-minded English empiricist breaking a lance for God, Harry, and the Cult of the Fact'.[1] So although, like *Contrary Imaginations*,

1. Worsley (1967).

this book is a research report, it moves – as the earlier work did not – towards a more general view of research and of human action.

Also my research has become more sociological, less exclusively psychological, in tone. Although I did not fully realize this at the time, *Contrary Imaginations* was in effect a comparison between two British sub-cultures. In studying the attraction of convergers towards science and divergers towards the arts, I was watching the crystallization of two contrasting ways of life.[2] Whether or not the present work achieves it, such a fusion of psychological and social modes of explanation is long overdue. Psychologists – especially British psychologists – still tend to take their stance with the biologists and assume that the causes of behaviour lie within the organism; while anthropologists and sociologists take it for granted that the roots of a human's actions are to be found in the roles and expectations of the social order that surrounds him. Psychologists have relied on the analogy of the billiard ball; social scientists on that of dough or putty.[3]

The rest of this book represents an effort to live this distinction down; to construct a framework of explanation that leaves one free to draw on both psychological and social forms of information – if not with equal facility, at least without embarrassment. Eventually this should lay the way open for a study of the human intellect in which the qualities of the individual and those of academic institutions – schools, universities, laboratories – are shown to interlock. The mental abilities and predispositions of the individual will be seen to evolve not *in vacuo* but in response to the demands that environments place upon him.

Conversely, the institutions will be seen not as arbitrary or

2. The reasons for my blindness now seem discreditable. I had assumed that any issue – such as the 'Two Cultures' – over which Lord Snow and Dr Leavis had done battle must be specious. Though useful, this rule-of-thumb has its exceptions.

3. These of course are caricatures; few of us would now be caught red-handed with either. None the less, most students of human behaviour originate on one side or other of this divide, and show a marked preference for one of the two analogies. There is no question here of reducing psychology to sociology, or vice versa. I merely wish to ignore a line of academic demarcation, as troublesome as it is arbitrary – to do not biological science, nor social science, but human science.

God-given, but as social mechanisms that individual men develop (and are continually changing) in order to fulfil their potentialities and to quiet their fears.

CHAPTER 2

RESPECT FOR AUTHORITY

IN this chapter and the next, I want to explore the relation of convergence and divergence to two other dimensions of psychological relevance: authoritarianism and masculinity. These dimensions were chosen not at random but on the strength of certain assumptions about the nature of mental life. The first of these concerns the relation of the individual to intellectual authority. I would argue that in all constructive brainwork, a tension exists between the need to innovate and the weight of established principle and precedent. Kuhn has pointed to this in scientific research:

... only investigations firmly rooted in the contemporary scientific tradition are likely to break that tradition and give rise to a new one. That is why I speak of an 'essential tension' implicit in scientific research. To do his job the scientist must undertake a complex set of intellectual and manipulative commitments. Yet his claim to fame, if he has the talent and good luck to gain one, may finally rest upon his ability to abandon this net of commitments in favour of another of his own invention. Very often the successful scientist must simultaneously display the characteristics of the traditionalist and of the iconoclast.[1]

The tension exists, likewise, in the literary and visual arts. One illustration will serve – from sculpture. Many would accept that the foremost sculptural innovator during the first half of this century has been the Rumanian peasant, Brancusi. As so often with great innovators, his early work was brilliant in technique but derivative in style. Particularly he was influenced by Rodin: Sleeping Muse One (1906), for instance, might well be a piece of Rodin's work. Rodin greatly admired Brancusi, and gave him the chance of working in his studio. Brancusi reluctantly turned the offer down and continued to work on his own – remarking, tradition has it, that 'nothing grows under big trees'. His later version of the Sleeping Muse theme – Sleeping

1. Kuhn (1963), p. 343.

Muse Two (1910), New Born (1915), Sculpture for the Blind (1924) – are works that Rodin could no sooner have produced than flown.

Both at school and at university this confrontation with intellectual authority is especially acute. It is made apparent to each of us, not through the malign motives of our teachers but from the force of our own ignorance, that if we want to succeed, our best course is to do what teachers and examiners expect of us. For this reason there exists a strong temptation not only to accept all authoritative judgements as given, but to accept the horizons of school and university syllabuses as the boundaries of all sensible inquiry. This massive largely unavoidable insistence on authoritative knowledge faces the student with an unenviable choice: that of knuckling under and being right; or of being individualistic, self-sufficient, and wrong.

The gist of my argument is that convergers and divergers will differ in their reaction to this dilemma. The first will tend to plump for those routes through the academic system – mathematics, physical science, classics – in which the weight of accepted authority is greatest; the second, those in which this pressure is least. What is alluring to the converger (and repugnant to the diverger) about the exact disciplines is their exactitude. They are systems of thought from which both muddle and emotion have largely been removed. This aspect of the difference between convergers and divergers is described in a phrase of Frenkel-Brunswik's:[2] convergers are 'intolerant of ambiguity' in intellectual matters, while divergers seem positively to seek it out. In their choice of a life's work convergers are drawn towards careers which hold the promise of crystalline exactitude and the ultimate exclusion of doubt. While for divergers, it is not only the emotional connotations of the arts that render them so attractive, but also their imprecision. V. S. Pritchett in his autobiography: 'The only certainty is that I come from a set of storytellers and moralists and that neither party cared much for the precise'.[3]

2. Frenkel-Brunswik (1950).
3. Pritchett (1968), p. 9.

The Authoritarian

For half a century or more, experimentally minded teachers and teachers' teachers have explored the influence on their pupils' judgement of an appeal to authoritative sources.[4] After the Second World War the topic gained a new direction and impetus from the atrocities of Nazi Germany, and research on 'authoritarianism' over the last two decades has primarily been concerned with political beliefs. Adorno and his colleagues, for example, sought to demonstrate that anti-Semitism was merely one aspect of a more general illiberality of attitude; that the 'authoritarian' also tended to value obedience and respect in children, to dislike introspection or the display of gentleness, to be superstitious, to believe in political toughness and power, to show a preoccupation with other people's sexual deviations, to spring from backgrounds which were both strict and socially insecure, to idealize his parents, and so on.[5]

After a wave of intense interest, this type of research has more recently fallen on hard times. The original study suffered technical defects which were seized upon by its critics, and a certain difficulty was found in the definition of authoritarianism itself. A number of commentators have suggested – justifiably in my view – that, politically speaking, there is an authoritarianism of the Left as well as of the Right, and for that matter of the Centre too. And Brown, at the end of a perspicacious review, argues that the true authoritarian is characterized not by the content of his beliefs, but by the kind of pressure that will induce him to change from one belief to another:

The authoritarian will reverse his evaluations on the simple say-so of an authority figure. If Stalin signs a pact with Berlin then Nazism becomes acceptable for the authoritarian Communist; if Krushchev devaluates Stalin the Communist authoritarian does the same. The authoritarian liberal would change his views on Communism if Franklin Roosevelt had told him to do so.... The non-authoritarian will also change his attitudes but the requisite information is

4. Asch (1955). In the late 1930s and 1940s a number of studies were done, too, on the effects of authoritarian, democratic and permissive regimes on groups of children. See e.g. Lewin, Lippitt and White (1939).

5. Adorno et al. (1950).

different. The endorsement of an authority will not be sufficient.[6]

This I take to be an important insight; and one which reconnects Adorno's research (although Brown does not seem to realize this) with the older tradition stemming from Thorndike and his generation, and now encompassing the work of Asch, Crutchfield and Milgram on 'yielding', and 'obedience'. Asch's experiments have demonstrated that in the face of pressure from a group of equals, some of us will deny the evidence of our senses – saying, for example, that manifestly the shorter of the two lines is the longer.[7] Such yielding, as Crutchfield and Milgram have shown, varies from one nation, even one occupation, to another: army officers and Norwegians, for instance, yield more readily than Frenchmen and research scientists.[8] And in the hands of Milgram, this tradition has blossomed (if so spring-like a verb is appropriate) into studies of obedience, in which ordinary citizens administer massive electric shocks to victims for no better reason than that a psychologist tells them to do so.[9]

Convergence and Yielding

In *Contrary Imaginations* I reported the tendency of convergers to adopt attitudes which I then called authoritarian. Convergers were more likely than divergers to approve of being obedient, and of having a low opinion of themselves, of accepting expert advice, and of having set opinions; and they were more likely to disapprove of being independent of their parents. Although overall the differences were statistically significant, item by item the differences were small. This authoritarianism on the part of convergers also extended to their attitudes about such issues as freedom in their choice of reading and compulsory membership of the Combined Cadet Force; and they were more likely to claim that they were happy at school.

6. Brown (1965).
7. Asch (1955).
8. Crutchfield (1962); Milgram (1961); see also Barron (1963).
9. Milgram (1965). The shocks of course are simulated; but those giving them do not realize this – as their own acute anxiety attests. Milgram's study suggests that such behaviour is 'normal' rather than the preserve of a pathologically sadistic minority.

Granted, then, that convergers tend to hold authoritarian attitudes; are they also authoritarian in the sense that they shift their ground under pressure? It was with this question of yielding that my first experiment was concerned. Studies of yielding traditionally involve an element of deception. The subjects of Asch's or Milgram's experiments are dupes, and they undergo (to put it no higher) embarrassment and discomfort. I find this unpalatable; so set myself to devise tests of yielding from which this element of deception was removed.[10] The first of these was based on a conventional questionnaire dealing with attitudes. Twenty-five multiple-choice questions were concocted more or less at random. In one question, for example, the individual was asked to choose the most appropriate name for characters in a television play; in another, the most likely number of motor cars on the road in the year 2000; in a third, the most suitable colour for a family saloon car. In each question he chose from among six alternatives.[11]

The first step was to classify a sample of forty-seven fifteen-year-old boys as convergers, all-rounders and divergers in the usual way.[12] These boys were then asked to complete the questionnaire. The differences between convergers' and divergers' responses proved (as I had hoped) to be slight and non-significant. Next, the same questionnaire was given to eighty university graduates. The third and crucial step was to rewrite the questionnaire, shuffling the six alternative answers to each question into a new order – one that reflected the opinions the graduate sample had expressed. With each question, the most popular answer among the graduates was now given as the first alternative; the second most popular was given as the second

10. Many problems in psychology lead the experimenter into trivial deception: he professes an interest in one variable while keeping his eye open for another. I do this continually. My objection is more specific: (a) to deception over matters of fact – e.g. presenting a poem by a schoolboy as one by Shakespeare; and (b) to embarrassment or humiliation, especially in front of an audience.

11. For a full description of this and other tests, see Appendix B.

12. Individuals are classified as convergers or divergers by means of their scores on an I Q test (A.H.5); and two open-ended tests, *Meanings of Words* and *Uses of Objects*. The convergers are those who are better at the I Q test than they are at the open-ended tests; the divergers are the reverse – stronger on the open-ended tests than on I Q. For a full description of the method, see Appendix A.

alternative; and so on down to the answer that the graduates had chosen least. Compare, for example, the original and revised lists of alternatives for 'the beautiful but foolish debutante' in a television play:

ORIGINAL	REVISED
(1) Clarissa	(1) Clarissa
(2) Hermione	(2) Alicia
(3) Anne	(3) Anne
(4) Alicia	(4) Hermione
(5) Patricia	(5) Sybil
(6) Sybil	(6) Patricia

Likewise, the two versions for 'the portly and slightly dishonest business tycoon who would like his son to marry the debutante':

ORIGINAL	REVISED
(1) Robins	(1) Bunton
(2) McCulloch	(2) Snyder
(3) Snyder	(3) Robins
(4) Jones	(4) Ramsbottom
(5) Bunton	(5) McCulloch
(6) Ramsbottom	(6) Jones

The instructions for the revised version of the questionnaire read as follows:

Obviously, there are no right answers. Each question is a matter of personal judgement. However, in making up your mind, you may like to take into account the opinions of other people. These same questions have recently been put to a large group of University graduates, and their answers are recorded for you to see. The alternative answers to each question have been arranged so that the first alternative is the most popular one among University gradua- tes, the second alternative is the second most popular, the third alternative is the third most popular, and so on. Thus, in Question 1, Clarissa is the most popular name for the foolish debutante, and Patricia is the least popular.

In its revised form, the questionnaire was then given to a fresh sample of fifteen-year-old boys. If respect for authority is a general quality of the convergent mind, one would expect that the convergers in this new sample would be more likely than the divergers to pick alternatives high on each list. And this, in fact, is what happened. Among those who yielded most, there were seventeen convergers and only seven divergers. Conversely, twenty-one divergers were among those who yielded least and only thirteen convergers. The discrimination, in other words, is respectable without being overwhelming.[13] The manoeuvre was then repeated on a further sample, this time of sixteen-year-old girls. The pattern followed by the girls' results echoed the boys' almost exactly: again, the convergers were more likely to yield, the divergers less.[14] This suggests that low mental fluency may well be linked to a more general susceptibility to pressure from authority: that the individual with a taste for the 'one right answer', both in answering mental tests and in his life's work, is particularly susceptible to information about what his elders and betters think correct.

Another experiment in this vein deserves a little space. It was based on six pieces of verse, and was designed to bring not one but a series of pressures to bear. Boys were asked to make two separate judgements: to express their personal preferences about the poems, and to judge their literary merit. As soon as they had committed themselves, an additional piece of information was passed to them, and they were asked to commit themselves again. The process was repeated three times in all. The first snippet of evidence gave the judgements of literary experts; the second the fact that three of the poems were by famous authors (Wordsworth, Byron, Macaulay), the other three by American schoolgirls. The third piece of evidence disclosed that all six

13. A point about statistics. We need to know two facts about any discrimination. First, what are the chances that it is a fluke? In this case, using the X^2 test, we find that the chances are less than 5 in 100: $P<0.05$. Second, we need some index of how *large* the discrimination is. How many exceptions are there to the rule that convergers yield more than divergers? No generally accepted method of doing this exists. As a rough guide, I calculate a proportion of 'sorts' (instances that fit the rule) to 'mis-sorts' (instances that contradict it): in this instance, $1.9:1$. So each discrimination mentioned in the text has two statistics appended to it in a footnote: (i) a proportion of sorts to missorts, and (ii) a statement of probability. Where necessary, the total number of individuals taking part in the experiment is given as well. In this case, $n=70$.

14. $2.3:1$, $P<0.025$, $n=117$.

were juvenilia – one, for instance, was written by a girl aged five. The first two pressures in other words, are pressures to yield; the third offers a mitigating circumstance.[15] The individual is free to stand fast, holding his original position unchanged; to yield; to rebel; or to change his judgements apparently haphazardly, to 'wander'.

The results were complicated by a difference between schools. The *Poems* were used at both a grammar and a public school, and boys from the first – arguably less self-confident – yielded much more than those from the second.[16] In their judgements of literary merit the public school convergers moved at once to the 'full yield' position; but subsequently 'wandered'. Public school divergers appeared not to yield at all; rather to 'wander' from the beginning. At the grammar school, the convergers not only moved straight to the 'full yield' position, but stuck there steadfastly throughout the remainder of the experiment; while grammar school divergers behaved like the public school convergers – they yielded fully at first, but subsequently drifted away again.

In their expressions of personal preference, as opposed to assessments of literary merit, convergers and divergers were more or less equally swayed by the authoritative view. More interesting was the tendency of divergers to link their judgements of personal preference and their judgements of merit together; whereas among convergers, especially early on in the test, these were clearly distinguished.[17] Also interesting in passing is the fact that while both disliked Byron, convergers were more enthusiastic than divergers about the patriotic effort by young Macaulay:

> *Remember the man who in sorrow and danger,*
> *When thy glory was set, and thy spirit was low,*
> *When thy hopes were o'erturned by the arms of the stranger,*
> *And thy banner displayed in the halls of the foe,*

15. The poems were taken from Terman's invaluable study of precocity (1930). The details of this particular experiment are complex and are described in Appendix B.

16. $3 \cdot 1:1$, $P < 0 \cdot 005$, $n = 91$.

17. $1 \cdot 9:1$, $P < 0 \cdot 1$. However, this may simply reflect divergers' greater self-confidence in literary matters.

Stood forth in the tempest of doubt and disaster,
Unaided and single, the danger to brave,
Asserted thy claims, and the rights of his master,
Preserved thee to conquer, and saved thee to save.

Divergers, on the other hand, were more appreciative of Wordsworth:

How pleasant, as the sun declines, to view
The spacious landscape change in form and hue!
Here, vanish, as in mist, before a flood
Of bright obscurity, hill, lawn, and wood;
There, objects, by the searching beams betrayed,
Come forth, and here retire in purple shade;
Even the white stems of birch, the cottage white,
Soften their glare before the mellow light . . .

The experiment is obviously at fault in failing to take differences in literary sophistication into account. If the subject-matter were more to convergers' taste, the relatively small differences between convergers and divergers (though not those between schools) might well be reversed. But the idea of sequential pressures none the less seems a good one, and worthy of elaboration.[18]

Sylbs and Sylfs

It has often been remarked that a prescribed syllabus can restrict the range of students' curiosity. Evidently, too, there is scope for individual differences in this matter. Some students bend their wits almost exclusively to getting good examination marks; others focus on the syllabus only with difficulty, and have intellectual interests that range far beyond it. The first – to coin a phrase – are 'syllabus-bound'; the second are 'syllabus-free'. The first group, the 'sylbs', accept the restrictions that a syllabus imposes; the 'sylfs' resent or ignore them.

The importance of this topic was suggested to me by a remark of a Cambridge psychiatrist. He had noticed that a frequent

18. The situations engineered by Asch and Milgram are also cumulative, of course, but lack variety.

cause of mental breakdown among Cambridge undergraduates seemed to be their discovery, for the first time in their lives, that they could not encompass the whole syllabus. They had no authoritative guidance about what to concentrate on, and what to ignore. At school, exhaustive coverage had been possible; now there was just too much to read – and hence the inherent risk of being examined on material for which they were unprepared. Relevant too are the observations made by Parlett, while watching a physics course at the Massachusetts Institute of Technology. The course was in the nature of an experiment; the instructor, a young professor, eager not merely to cram his audience with information for their quizzes and examinations, but to give them a grasp of the more fundamental issues at stake. When the occasion merited it, he would digress, and talk about matters not in the syllabus:

On one such occasion there was a highly significant interruption. The instructor had begun to speak about Einstein's dispute with other physicists over the probabilistic treatment of quantum mechanics and was reading short extracts from a book about Einstein. One student raised his hand, took it down, raised it again. The instructor, who was engrossed in his description, did not at first notice. When he did, he stopped what he was saying – almost in mid-sentence – and said 'Yes?'[19]

The student's question had nothing to do with Einstein, or even with physics. Only – 'Have you marked the quiz?'

One wonders immediately, are syllabus-bound students convergers? My part in answering this question was to construct a syllabus-bound/syllabus-free questionnaire; a collection of items about the attitudes of the individual to his work. From an original list of twenty-four, nine items were found to cluster together satisfactorily, and form a 'sylb/sylf' scale:

I tend to be erratic, sometimes working well, sometimes badly.
I think that my school marks are a fairly accurate reflection of my
    true ability.
Interests out of school often make me neglect my work.
I like teachers who stick to the syllabus, and do not digress.

19. Parlett (1967). Dr Parlett and I have worked together on 'sylbs' and 'sylfs', and I am indebted to him.

*I find schoolwork restricting and would like to have more choice in
what I study.*
I would rather pursue my own ideas than follow a syllabus.
I wish schoolwork was less trivial.
I often disagree with my teachers.
*I find that I work hard when I am interested and slack when I
am not.*

Preliminary results from sixteen-year-old boys suggest that
convergers are indeed more syllabus-bound than divergers.[20] In
general, it seems, the converger largely accepts what the school
has to offer; the diverger is less satisfied, wider ranging, and
liable to find schoolwork trivial or tiresome. Analogous differences have been found among American ten-year-olds. Wallach
and Kogan conclude that divergers are often children 'in conflict
with school and with themselves', while convergers have a
relationship to school that is 'addictive': 'A logic has been
established wherein academic success is the path to all things of
significance and value, while academic failure is tantamount to
complete destruction.'[21] It is particularly interesting to learn
that at MIT, where by English standards supervision is
claustrophobically close, it is apparently the 'sylfs' not the
'sylbs' who fall into psychiatric difficulties.[22]

One might also have predicted that the converger's acceptance
of the school regime (and the diverger's rejection of it) would
have an effect on the work habits of the boys concerned: that
convergers would be neat and well-organized; divergers slap-
dash. In fact, the evidence tells against this. The original list of
twenty-four items contained seven referring directly to study
habits; only one turned out to have even a tangential connection
with the nine items in the 'sylb/sylf' scale. In this respect,
differences between convergers and divergers were slight and
inconsistent.[23] Attitudes to authority and to school regime are

20. $3 \cdot 0 : 1$, $P < 0 \cdot 05$, n=43. Two items were particularly discriminative. *Interests
out of school often make me neglect my work* and *I wish schoolwork was less trivial*; $2 \cdot 5 : 1$
and $2 \cdot 4 : 1$ respectively, $P < 0 \cdot 005$.

21. Wallach and Kogan (1965). p. 285.

22. Snyder (1967); Parlett (1967).

23. A similar division between general attitudes to work and specific study habits
was found by Parlett among undergraduates at MIT; Parlett (1967).

both linked it seems, to convergence and divergence; but the network of correlates does not encompass the more specific tactics the individual employs in coping with his academic work. The boy who claims to like teachers who stick to the syllabus is no more likely than any other to keep his notes in logical order, do his written work in good time, or avoid careless mistakes.[24]

Conscientiousness

Reading the items in the 'sylb/sylf' scale, one senses that the syllabus-bound boy must have about him a distinct air of dutifulness. He can scarcely be a swashbuckler, and he may even be 'good'. His form-mates probably tend to see him as conscientious. Is this also true of the converger? Conversely, are divergers seen as rebellious and intellectually independent? It is a simple enough matter to check.

So far, the work has been done only on samples of girls.[25] Among them, convergers do tend to be picked out as conscientious; and the divergers as rebellious and intellectually independent. However, these differences are virtually swamped – and for the second time in a chapter – by a difference between the two schools taking part. One, a grammar school, caters for girls from predominantly lower-middle and middle-class homes; the other, a public school in a fashionable London suburb, takes a substantial proportion of its children from the professional upper-middle class. The schools also appear to differ in their general atmosphere; the grammar school placing great emphasis on good manners and self-control, the public school slightly less. Perhaps as a result of these differences, the grammar-school girls proved more likely than public-school girls to nominate their convergent form-mates – irrespective of the quality under consideration. Grammar-school girls tended to

24. One is reminded of Charles Dickens; a man of remarkable intellectual fertility, but obsessively tidy in his working habits – 'keep things in their places. I can't bear to picture them otherwise.' Hibbert (1967).

25. Six qualities were used for these form-mates' ratings: most conscientious, most eager to get good marks in examinations, most intellectually independent, most widely read outside the syllabus, most rebellious, least interested in school-work.

nominate convergers for virtues and vices alike; the public-school girls to nominate divergers.[26]

The implication is that either the social background of a school or its climate (or both) helps to determine whether convergers or divergers are in the public eye. A lower-middle class and seemingly more regimented school throws the converger forward and leaves the diverger anonymous; an upper-middle class and slightly more expansive one does the reverse. This finding, reflecting the impact of the social context on individuals of different intellectual types, has many echoes in what follows.[27]

The Man and Boy

Before leaving the theme of authority – to return soon enough – there is one last piece of work to mention. Promising but inconclusive, it bears on authoritarianism from a different point of view. Convergers and divergers were shown a picture of an 'authority situation', vaguely depicted, and allowed to interpret it however they saw fit. The picture showed a middle-aged Man sitting behind a desk or table; and standing facing him a young Boy. The Man and the Boy were rated in terms of ten pairs of adjectives; boys were asked to say, for example, whether the Man seemed 'friendly' or 'unfriendly'; 'worried' or 'unworried'. They were then invited to describe in their own words what was going on.

The simple-minded prediction here is quite clear: convergers will be more likely to see the situation as involving the exercise of authority or punishment, divergers to construe it as one of solicitude or advice. Convergers will see the Man as stern, the divergers as benign. The converger should differentiate clearly between superior and inferior figures in the authority situation, and see them as embodying different qualities; the diverger should see them as confused. There is, however, a more subtle

26. $1\cdot8:1$, $P < 0\cdot05$, n=117.
27. Unfortunately, these studies were not designed with differences between schools in mind. One consequence is that in all my evidence about girls, social class and the atmosphere or climate of a school are confounded.

prediction, and one which half contradicts the first. The converger, precisely because he accepts authority, is less likely than the diverger to be disturbed by it. The diverger, conversely, still raw and unreconciled, is more likely to react uneasily. On this second argument it is the converger who should see both figures as belonging harmoniously to a single system of authority, while the diverger should see them as openly opposed.

Although far from decisive, the results seem to support the second, subtle prediction rather than the first simple one. Convergers do certainly seem more likely than divergers to see the scene as an exercise of authority; they see the Man as punishing the Boy, for example, whereas divergers see him as bringing influence or persuasion to bear.[28] And the convergers are also more likely to see the Man as a schoolmaster; the divergers as the Boy's father.[29] But, on the other hand, divergers are more likely than convergers to see the Man as in some sense menacing: as 'hard' as opposed to 'soft'; as 'strong' as opposed to 'weak'; as 'unfriendly' as opposed to 'friendly'.[30] Divergers also tend to describe the Man as 'dull', whereas convergers see him as 'exciting'.[31]

The most interesting detail is the differentiation of the character of the Boy from that of the Man. Divergers give the Man and Boy quite distinctive personalities; convergers see the two personalities as fairly similar.[32] There seems, in other words, to be confirmation in this small experiment for the general argument of this chapter: that the converger is more likely to see ordinary social situations in terms of authority, but – precisely because he lives within an authoritarian frame of reference – is less likely than the diverger to see authority figures as threatening. He accepts the authority of older men, and because he accepts it,

28. 2·7:1, P <0·1, n=43. Tested at one school only.
29. 2·1:1, P <0·01.
30. 1·7:1, 1·6:1, 1·7:1, respectively. In each case, P <0·1.
31. 2·8:1, P <0·1.
32. 2·0:1, P <0·1. This distinction is more marked when – as in Chapter 6 – we base convergence and divergence on boys' self-estimate : 3·0:1, P <0·05. It might be argued that divergers are simply more perceptive about people than convergers, or more interested in interpreting vague pictures. Yet in another test of this type, depicting not a Man and Boy but Man and Woman, this difference between convergers and divergers disappears. See Chapter 3.

is not agitated. Evidently, though, as the modest size of the relationships throughout this chapter shows, there is more to convergence than the acceptance of authority – and more to divergence than its rejection. Authoritarianism and convergence overlap; they do not coincide.

MASCULINE AND FEMININE

THERE are good grounds for believing that two of the earliest categories assimilated by a child are those of masculinity and femininity;[1] and good grounds, too, for believing that many of us never quite satisfy ourselves that we belong wholly to one category or the other. Hence masculinity and femininity can be seen not as two distinct biological categories (open to the occasional hermaphroditic exception), but as a spectrum stretching from one extreme to the other, and on which the positions of those who are biologically male and female are sometimes confused. The individual is placed on this spectrum not by medical examination, but by question about his interests and attitudes, or by observation of his behaviour, or by his perception of his own character. We are dealing, in other words, not in anatomy, nor even in the perception of anatomy, but in personality and the perception of personality. Before setting to work with a dimension that may still seem a little insubstantial, I shall first bed it down in some evidence from biology and social anthropology.

Some Anthropological Evidence

The first principle of social anthropology – as familiar now as it was once startling – is that there are no universal laws of human behaviour. Actions natural in one society are often unnatural in another. To accept this, however, is not to lapse into complete cultural relativism. There are statistical regularities in the evidence about primitive peoples that are of more interest perhaps to psychologists than they are to anthropologists themselves. Just as among the monkeys and the great apes, so among humans, there are unmistakable signs of sexual

1. Kohlberg (1967), who discusses a considerable body of evidence about sex discriminations in young children.

'dimorphism': not merely in physique but in social behaviour.[2]

In almost every society that anthropology has yet embraced, men have been found to specialize in certain skills and areas of responsibility, women in others. D'Andrade claims, for example, that in a sample of 224 economically primitive societies there is not one in which the women usually or always do the hunting; conversely, there are only six in which the grinding of corn is usually or always done by the men.[3] Statistically speaking, herding, fishing and clearing the ground for agriculture are dominated by men; carrying water, cooking, gathering roots and seeds, the preservation of meat and fish, and gathering fuel, tend to be the monopoly of women. In manufacture similar divisions occur. Metal-working, weapon-making, boat-building, the manufacture of musical instruments, work in wood, stone or bone, are with the rarest exceptions a masculine preserve; while the manufacture and repair of clothing, pottery-making, weaving, mat-making, basket-making, and manufacture of thread, is work usually done by women.

Analogous differences have been reported from the Israeli Kibbutzim; institutions in which women were explicitly and totally emancipated from their traditional position of domesticity and subservience.[4] Among the first settlers, there was no division of labour; men and women alike drove tractors, cooked and laundered. Yet it seems that a division has occurred. The men have gradually tended to specialize in the productive branches of the economy, the women in the service branches – that is, in cooking, cleaning, laundering, teaching, and caring for children.

The evidence suggests a natural polarity of the sexes.[5] There

2. DeVore (1965) notes that among old-world monkeys, males are larger and stronger than females, and from an early age more given to rough and tumble play. They also defend the group, and settle internal disputes. Analogous differences in pattern of play have been observed among human infants, e.g. by Blurton Jones (1967).

3. D'Andrade (1967), whose data are based on the earlier cross-cultural work of Murdock. This kind of ethnographic evidence is susceptible to distortions and inaccuracies of several kinds, but is of interest none the less.

4. Spiro (1956).

5. To say that a phenomenon is 'natural' is to admit neither that it is desirable nor unalterable. War and economic exploitation, cancer and syphilis are all 'natural' in this sense; none is self-evidently either desirable or unalterable.

is a tendency in most (but not all) societies for men to become the economic providers, while women's responsibilities are domestic. D'Andrade's tables also make it clear that associated with this economic distinction is one of personality, the male tending to be aggressive, and women nurturative.[6] Reworking his statistics one finds, too, a marked tendency for societies to polarize their activities in one direction or the other.[7] There is a tendency, in other words, for a primitive society to award its activities either to men or to women exclusively.

This distinction of sex roles is linked in its turn with the subject of the previous chapter: authority. There are few societies, it seems, in which wives are explicitly claimed to exercise greater social authority than husbands – even in the home. D'Andrade quotes a study of 31 societies: the husband was said in 21 of these, to exercise authority over the wife; in six their spheres of authority were claimed to be different; and only in four did the wife appear to have more *de facto* authority within the family than the husband.[8]

The Arts and Sciences

What is particularly interesting about this anthropological evidence is the way in which considerations of authority and masculinity influence activities where biological differences between men and women would seem irrelevant: weapon-making, for instance, and bearing burdens.[9] A parallel in our

6. In sociological terms, the man is instrumental, the woman expressive. Parsons and Shils (1951).

7. Each of 42 activities is classified as 'men always', 'men usually', 'either sex', 'women usually', 'women always'. The number of societies mentioned under the two extreme categories ('men always' and 'women always') heavily outweighs that placed in the other three: 3·4:1, P <0·001. The proportion of completely polarized activities to those which are not polarized at all (the 'either sex' category) is even higher: 7·8:1, P <0·001. D'Andrade goes on to argue that there is 'a complete network of relationships between division of labour by sex, subsistence activities, and types of social organization'. D'Andrade (1967).

8. Stephens (1963). Whether these claims reflect actual practice remains a little unclear. One of the four possible exceptions were the Tchambuli of New Guinea. But even among the Tchambuli, men appear to have greater authority than women in groups larger than the family.

9. D'Andrade's figures indicate that there are four to five societies in which women bear burdens to every one in which men do so.

own society would seem to be the arts and the sciences. There is evidence that scientists are seen (and see themselves) as a group embodying – in Angus Wilson's phrase – that 'masculinity demanded conventionally in our own day of those who call themselves men'.[10] To a greater extent than his counterpart in the arts the scientist has interests, attitudes and pastimes that our society deems to be eminently male.[11] He is also more likely to be muscular in physique.[12]

There is an overwhelming preponderance of males in the physical sciences; the proportion of men to women in the Royal Society, for instance, is over 40 to 1.[13] Klein's figures indicate that among British doctors this proportion is between 4 and 5 to 1; among professional chemists it is at least 30 to 1; among physicists, 55 to 1; among electrical engineers, over 500 to 1; and among mechanical engineers, over 1,500 to 1.[14] It can be argued – with justice – that such male preponderance is heavily culturally determined. Reliable figures for the U.S.S.R. are hard to find, but estimates suggest that Russian women play a greater part in, for example, medicine and engineering than they do in this country or the United States. Even so, the differentiation between male 'instrumentality' and female 'expressivity' or 'nurturance' still seems to obtain. It has been suggested that as many as a third of Russia's professional engineers are women; on the other hand, the proportion of women who are doctors – a nurturative profession almost by definition – is said to be as high as three-quarters.[15]

10. Wilson (1967), p. 206.
11. McClelland (1962).
12. Parnell (1958); Seltzer (1948).
13. Hudson (1966a).
14. Klein (1966).
15. Degler (1964), Dornbusch (1967). These estimates, however, should be viewed with circumspection.

The Origins of Masculinity and Femininity

The evidence so far deals with broad differences between men and women, and says nothing about the origins of relative degrees of masculinity or femininity among men – or, for that matter – among women. Biological evidence suggests that such male qualities as aggressiveness may be linked in a fairly straight-forward manner with an individual's hormonal balance. Males of many species live in social hierarchies, in which the high-ranking males have rights of precedence to space, food and females. A number of studies show that if a low-ranking male is given injections of male sex hormone, he fights his way up to a higher position.[16] Further, female rhesus monkeys whose mothers have been given injections of male sex hormone during pregnancy, themselves grow up more aggressive than normal for the female rhesus.[17]

It has long been known that adolescent boys tend to be better than girls at mathematics, and worse verbally. This difference, though not massive, turns up fairly consistently whenever large samples of boys and girls are compared.[18] This, again, might be accountable in terms of differences in the secretion of sex hormones, or even of brain structure. More likely, though, is an explanation in terms of social roles: it may simply arise because, for reasons rational or irrational, mathematics is culturally defined as a man's world. On this argument – the 'social-learning hypothesis' – the individual gradually settles himself into the niche that the culture provides. An alternative and far riskier explanation hinges on the notion of identification. This asserts that the development of the individual is determined by relation-ships he forms as an infant with his parents: that psychic events occur in the nursery, long before the child has mastered language or any knowledge of social niches or roles, which will determine

16. Hamburg and Lunde (1967).
17. Young, Goy and Phoenix (1964). Bloom's (1964) evidence shows that whether determined genetically or by early environment, the amount of aggressiveness or dependency that an adolescent human displays can be predicted with surprising accuracy from observations made during the first five years of life.
18. Maccoby (1967).

to a considerable extent the niches and roles that he will later feel free to fill.[19]

In a study I envy, Carlsmith was able to examine the second of these interpretations by means of a natural experiment.[20] During the Second World War large numbers of normal young American males were drafted into the Armed Forces, and some left behind wives who were pregnant or who had very young children. By the early 1960s, these children had themselves grown up and some of the boys among them were undergraduates at Harvard. Carlsmith took note of their mathematical and verbal abilities, and found that these young men lacked the characteristic male bias towards mathematical reasoning. This deficit was particularly marked among those whose fathers had been away from home for the first two to three years of their children's lives.

This startling discovery cannot be explained away as a statistical fluke; superficially at least it is at odds with the 'social-learning hypothesis'; and it fits the 'identification hypothesis' to perfection.[21] Psychoanalytic theory holds that we identify ourselves with the figures we fear; and thereby fear them no longer. We model ourselves on the parent who punishes us.[22] Supportive evidence has been published more recently by Nelsen and Maccoby.[23] They found that male undergraduates with the characteristically 'female' pattern of mental ability – high verbal, low numerical – often reported that their fathers had been away from home for long periods, and that they had been punished exclusively by their mothers. The 'male' pattern in

19. 'Social-learning' and 'identification' hypotheses are of course complementary rather than mutually exclusive. Their emphasis nevertheless is different: one on rational understanding, and on the later years of childhood; the other on fantasies, and on the first two or three years of life. Both forms of explanation are alarmingly vague. See Winch (1962); Sears et al. (1966).

20. Carlsmith (1964).

21. On two matched subsamples of 20 each, Carlsmith achieved a discrimination of $3\cdot4{:}1$, $P < 0\cdot001$. In practice, of course, it is arguable that the absence of the father may have had a long-term effect on the quality of the marriage; and that this did not have its crucial influence on the child until, say, early adolescence.

22. Erikson (1963); Sears et al. (1966).

23. Nelsen and Maccoby (1966).

young men – low verbal and high numerical – is associated with punishment exclusively by the father. Again results fit the 'identification hypothesis'. The pattern of ability here described as 'female' is one strongly associated in English sixth forms and universities with specialization in the arts; the 'male' with science.[24]

Interesting results come, too, from Vernon's studies of verbal and non-verbal reasoning among Eskimos, Canadian Indians and Jamaicans.[25] While the young Eskimo boys, and to a lesser extent the young Canadian Indians, showed the characteristically male bias towards non-verbal reasoning, the young Jamaicans did not. He also found that among Canadian Indians this non-verbal ability was most marked in communities farthest removed from white civilization. Vernon's inference is that skill in non-verbal reasoning is developed by an upbringing that encourages the masculine virtues – in this case of hunting and trapping; and that is sapped by a way of life in which the men (as with Jamaicans and some Indians) are reduced to economic impotence.

In summary, therefore, there seems every indication that masculinity and femininity are pervasive characteristics of life in most human societies, if not in all, and that they may permeate not only an individual's interests, attitudes and choice of career, but also the patterning of his intelligence.[26] The obvious inference is that convergers will turn out to be more masculine than divergers. In practice, and especially at first, positive evidence of such a connexion proved hard to find.

Convergence and Divergence Among Girls

The first step in relating masculinity to convergence was to give open-ended tests to girls. Two factual matters were at issue. Were girls more divergent than boys? Were girls who specialized

24. Hudson (1960, 1966a). Also relevant is Milton's (1957) finding that masculinity of attitude and interest are positively related to skill in convergent problem solving.

25. Vernon (1965a, 1965b, 1966).

26. This is not to say that the attributes of masculinity or femininity are the same in all cultures; nor that one society's perception of masculinity and femininity in another may not suffer from ethnocentric bias.

in the arts more divergent than girls who specialized in physical science? On the assumption of some general connexion between mental fluency, the arts and femininity, one would certainly have expected the answer in both cases to be 'yes'.

With these questions in mind, I tested lower sixth form girls at two schools, one a grammar school, one a member of the Girls' Public Day School Trust. The comparison with my sample of boys was quite close: the coverage in terms of social class, age, intelligence quotient and academic ability being roughly the same. It was clear at once that the boys and girls in my sample differed in their fluency on a test like *Uses of Objects* – and in a direction I had not foreseen. It was the boys who were substantially the more fluent.[27] Boys and girls differed too in the quality of the responses they gave, boys for instance expressing more violence.

The relation of convergence and divergence to arts/science specialization among girls proved far from clear-cut. As with boys, divergent girls tend to avoid science subjects; but convergent girls are equally likely to go into the arts or physical science.[28]

The interpretation of psychological differences between girls and boys is notoriously awkward; the further one looks, the more apparent contradictions there are.[29] In this case, however, there is at least one factor of obvious relevance: the girls' social context. This seems to condition both their fluency on open-ended tests, and also the career choice they are free to make. The public school girls were significantly more fluent than the grammar school girls.[30] Even so, the public school girls were still not

27. When the comparison is restricted to boys and girls at neighbouring grammar schools, 2·4:1, P <0·001, n=54 and 80 respectively.

28. The proportion of divergent girls doing arts to those doing science is 3·0:1. Overall, though, the relation of convergence/divergence to arts/science specialization is weak, 1·5:1, P <0·1. Almost all of the girls taking physical science subjects were also taking biology. Consequently, a straightforward comparison with specialization among boys is impossible. Convergent boys are 3–4 times more likely to go into physical science than into the arts. Hudson (1966a).

29. For a survey of an impenetrably complex literature, see Maccoby (1967).

30. 1·6:1, P <0·025, n=119. One is tempted to interpret this quite simply as due to social class. In fact though the equivalent difference between grammar and public school boys tends to run the other way. The grammar school boys in my sample were

as fluent as boys. In Canada and Australia the same appears to be true – but not, it seems, in America where differences in fluency between boys and girls are slight.[31]

The draconian quality of girls' education in this country may help to explain both this and another aspect of girls' responses. In scoring *Uses of Objects*, I use a category labelled 'sex and smut', but which is usually filled (as on this occasion) with the mildest innuendoes. Surprisingly, girls produced more of these than boys.[32] Specifically, girls were more likely than boys to make the following suggestions for a telegraph pole:

> Piss-post for dogs.
> Dogs.
> For dogs when they feel the need.
> Convenient post for dogs.
> Sanitation for dogs.
> Place at which dogs can leave landmarks for finding their way home.
> For dogs (it saves trees).
> For animals to use to go to the toilet behind.
> Useful for male dogs.
> For the convenience of dogs when lamposts become extinct.

These responses were much more frequent among girls at what I judged to be the more repressive grammar school; and it may be that they were a by-product of that repression.[33] Why girls otherwise should show a preoccupation with the urino-genital habits of male dogs I cannot fathom.

The bearing of their academic setting on girls' career choice is more direct. In England, as in America, girls who specialize in physical science are the exception. It follow that those girls who take the plunge into physical science will tend to have both natural gifts in this direction and considerable independence of

---

the more fluent of the two. Their school regime however seemed exceptionally libertarian – and it is this, I think, that will eventually prove crucial.

31. Wallach and Kogan (1965); Cropley and Field (1968); Maccoby (1967).

32. When neighbouring grammar schools were compared, 1·8:1, P <0·05, n=133.

33. 8·0:1, P <0·01. The influence of social class and school climate cannot be disentangled without using a wide cross-section of schools; and also some objective measure of institutional control. See, e.g., Lambert *et al.* (1968).

judgement. We already know that convergent girls tend to lack independence of judgement. The convergent girl is thus caught in two fires: her ability and temperament draw her towards science, while her respect for conventional wisdom draws her away. On this argument, one would expect what one finds: that there is no clear connexion between convergence and specialization in science among girls; that the situation is confused.[34]

Before I leave my sample of girls, I should like to record one last piece of evidence about them. It is paradoxical, and I offer it without any clear idea of where it might lead. Convention holds that men and women have distinct social roles. Yet girls who display marked independence of judgement – who do not yield on the tests described in Chapter 2 – are much more likely than other girls to *approve* of a clear distinction between the behaviour appropriate to girls and to boys.[35] The girls who do not yield are those who say that the following activities are suitable either for boys or for girls, but not for both: having an active interest in politics, swearing, mending clothes, getting drunk, cooking, enjoying war films, hitch-hiking, visiting pubs alone, owning a sports car, and looking after young children. It seems that girls who have independence of judgement are less 'emancipated' than those who lack it. I can only assume that Emancipation for Women has now become an orthodoxy, and that those who think for themselves are moving back towards a conception of male and female lives as distinct (although not necessarily of different status). Although tangential to the main theme of my research, this result seems worth pursuing.

The Man and The Woman

Evidently differences in fluency between the biologically male and the biologically female are confused with questions of social context and expectation. Although interesting in their own right, they reveal little about shades of masculinity and femininity

34. One would also predict that girls find it difficult to sustain a career in physical science, being prone to move away into biological and social science, or into teaching. Also that the feminine approach to arts subjects would often embody much of the precision that one associates with the convergent male.

35. This difference is a solid one: $3\cdot3:1$, $P < 0.025$, $n = 119$.

within one sex. The last two studies in this chapter deal more directly with this theme, and are in the nature of preliminary sorties. One worked well initially, but later ran into complications; the other was perhaps too crudely designed ever to deserve much success.

The first of these resembled the 'Man and Boy' study mentioned towards the end of Chapter 2, but was based on a picture of a Man and a Woman. Boys were asked to respond to them in the style of the *Semantic Differential*,[36] rating the two figures on pairs of adjectives; and then by sketching out a brief narrative plot involving the Man or the Woman or both. The Man was a rather gloomy, middle-aged Edwardian figure; the Woman much younger and uneasy-looking, even mildly distraught. Convergers tended consistently to take a less favourable view of the Woman than they did of the Man: they tended to see her as less wholesome, exciting, unworried, strong and safe. Divergers did the reverse.[37]

In writing stories about the Man and Woman convergers tended to restrict themselves to action and high adventure, and avoided more personal matters.[38] Consider these plots, the first three by extreme convergers – the third not entirely original:

The man has discovered that his daughter, the woman, has stolen some money, but he does not know whom she has taken it from. So he takes it from her secretly and puts it on a rock off the coast of Ireland, where they are staying. As the boat leaves with him and the daughter, he looks at the rock, which he has arranged to blow up as they leave. The daughter knows his plan and has taken the money from the rock, and looks at her father with distrust. The rock blows up and both are satisfied; father because he thinks he has cheated his daughter of her stolen money, and daughter because she has the money all the time.

He is a scientist, he discovered a new element in 1835. She is his wife but they don't particularly like each other. He is an upright perfect man, who is always punktual. She is fairly rich and so is he, they have a mansion in London. His laboratory is somewhere else for he always

36. See Appendix B. The *Semantic Differential* is discussed at length in Chapters 4 and 5.
37. Cumulatively this difference was significant, $1\cdot3:1$, $P < 0\cdot005$, $n = 72$.
38. $1\cdot6:1$, $P < 0\cdot05$.

sets off to his research work at 8.00 in the morning. She hates someone
– Not him.

Her two brothers killed each other in combat. One was allowed to be
buried by her uncle the king. The other had to decay outside the wall
of the city. Anyone caught burying her other brother would be killed.
She did so, and her uncle much to his despair had to order the death
sentence on her.

Now three by extreme divergers:

Man attracted to another woman, but he is married to this one, who
though rather sweet, unexciting. Man does not really want to hurt her
feelings, so supposedly gets himself killed and goes off with the rich
miss X. His wife is left the money and moderately happy looking after
there 1 son. After a couple of years the floosie gets sick of her rather
dull companion, and casts him by the way side. He is now worried
because practically penny less, and accustomed to the good life, he is
preparing to go and tell his wife the truth, because he believes she will
take him back.

Man and wife. Man married when much older than woman. Woman
at first adored man. Then he suddenly became a clergyman and seemed
to get older. Woman's interest in man declined. Man loved woman v.
strongly but not vice versa. Woman meets another man. Falls in love,
feels guilty, 1st man finds out, heartbroken, woman loses interest in
other man, feels very sorry for man (1st) but cannot love him. Man
will not be reconciled with woman. Divorce. Man goes on preaching,
then dies at 75. Woman meanwhile, living by herself, takes to drink,
goes rather mad, very depressed, commits suicide.

I would have said that the two are husband and wife, had once seen
better times, gone down in the world, the husband had inherited a lot
of goods he had been swindled, as he is rather weak minded, his wife,
rules the roost. Both are ageing, and have nothing to look forward to
but an early death. They are no longer particularly fond of each other
and every day is a trial. She cannot do anything about it as she is
helpless in the world without his moral support.

Convergers were also less likely to suggest a specifically sexual
relationship between the two figures; to mention the topic of
suicide; and to suggest that the two figures differed in social
class. Convergers tended, on the other hand, to describe scenes
of victimization and intrigue – in which, for instance, the man

blackmails the woman or vice versa; and to tell a story in which
only one of the two figures plays a part. Taken one by one these
differences are not statistically significant, but the picture which
emerges from them is consistent.

So far, so good. There is a snag, however. When I repeated
this experiment on a similar group, but using boys' estimates of
their own convergence or divergence as my criterion rather than
their actual test scores, all the differences just mentioned
disappeared.[39] Clearly, there is an important distinction to be
drawn here between the 'actual' and the 'perceived', between a
boy's perception of his own abilities and the abilities he in fact
possesses. This distinction is explored at length in the chapters
that follow.

Some Other Variables

A similar air of initial interest and subsequent puzzlement
attaches itself to the next set of results. The *Man and Woman*
test, combining the projective method with a rigorous scaling
of responses, was quite subtle; by comparison the second study
was blunt in the extreme. Rosenberg has found that complex
relationships exist between birth order, and 'self-image' –
between a boy's position in the family and certain judgements he
makes about himself and his relationships with other people.[40]
My adaptation of his method led to the analysis of a dozen or
more variables, including 'perceived' and 'actual' convergence/
divergence. And the theme of sex identification was tackled head
on: each boy was asked, quite simply, to say whether he thought
he more closely resembled his mother or his father; and also to
say which parent, if he had the choice, he would like to resemble
more than he now did.[41]

I had half hoped, naïvely, that convergers might be more
willing than divergers to liken themselves to their fathers. In

39. This method is described in Chapter 6.

40. Rosenberg (1965).

41. Psychoanalysts point out, rightly, that sexual identity is a topic on which many
people are touchy and self-deceptive; and hence that any results from the 'head-on'
approach are bound to be virtually meaningless. Granted this objection, the direct
method is often worth trying, if only to see what kind of touchiness and self-deception
results.

practice, convergers' and divergers' responses were in this respect virtually indistinguishable. Another variable in the analysis concerned 'faith-in-people' – an idea derived directly from Rosenberg. My prediction was that divergers, though more interested in people than convergers, would prove less trustful of them. On the first sample tested, this turned out to be so; on the second, the difference disappeared. Among other variables explored were family size and birth order: neither produced significant results. In fact, the only plum to emerge from this doughy pudding was a relationship with little bearing on convergers and divergers. Boys from families of one or two children were nearly twice as likely as those from large families to say that they resembled their mothers.[42] The same is true to a slightly lesser extent of only sons and eldest sons. Also boys from small families were less likely than other boys to say that they would like to be more like their fathers. They usually equivocated, or (which was relatively unusual) chose their mothers. This apart, the analysis had little to offer.

A Strategic Point

Before launching into further studies of boys' perceptions – of the arts and sciences and of themselves – I should like briefly to take stock. Chapter 2 made it clear that a connexion exists between convergence and respect for authority; also that this connexion is not a close one. Chapter 3, on the strength of other people's evidence rather than my own, suggests that there is probably a similar connexion between convergence and masculinity: substantial but not close. Is the slackness of the connexions between these three variables – the fact that convergence, respect for authority and masculinity do no more than overlap – a source for alarm?

I do not think so. Quite the reverse, in fact. In practice there is every reason to believe that the human personality is organized in terms not of a single major variable or dimension or polarity, but many. And that the inconsistencies apparent in human action arise not only from the complexity of the personality structure

42. $1 \cdot 9 : 1$, P $< 0 \cdot 05$, n$=86$.

that underlies them, but from at least three further sources: (i) the influence on behaviour of human perception and self-perception; (ii) the influence of specific social and psychological contexts; and (iii) the possibility of interactions between all the relevant variables – basic personality structure, perception, and social context – which are themselves complex. We normally assume that such relationships are roughly linear, and additive in their effect. There is no reason though why human nature should be organized in ways that are statistically convenient.

It follows that there is little point for the psychologist in blindly correlating one variable with another. Far-flung networks of correlation are not enough: because they run thin; because they excite an interest in causal processes they are rarely able to satisfy; and, overwhelmingly, because human beings are manifestly consistent only over a relatively narrow range of situations. This is not to say that every man is a law unto himself, nor that the workings of the human mind are at root capricious. It is precisely because one assumes that inconsistencies are lawful and capriciousness apparent, that the argument runs as it does. If we fail to find correlations between variables which we feel in our bones (or on other good grounds) are causally related, we need not despair. Our failure serves to show only that the particular variables are not related in any gross or simple way; that our logical model is too elementary; and that we would be wise to approach next time by another route. It is just this that I attempt next.

CHAPTER 4

THE MYTHS OF ARTS AND SCIENCE

KANT pointed out, like others before and since, that we do not merely perceive the world about us, we *order* it. Sense data do not flow through our minds in a random flood; we filter, select, discriminate. Imposed automatically, this filtering is at times rational and adaptive; at others, a penumbra of prejudice and intuition, which can be rational or adaptive only in some more subtle sense. Psychologists often assume (as I do) that it is the less rational-seeming of these filtering processes that exert a dominant influence over our behaviour day by day, influencing the choices we make, trivial and more committing – of a car, a house, a painting, a wife, a profession. It is into this penumbra that I now propose to delve.

It is clear in particular that we do not perceive the professions in any simple or straightforward fashion. Especially is this true of the arts and sciences. The topic has been explored experimentally; Beardslee and O'Dowd, for instance, summarize the American student's view of the scientist in the following terms:

First, the scientist is characterized by high intelligence dissociated from artistic concerns and sensitivities. . . . Second, there is a clear lack of interest in people . . . self-sufficient, rational, persevering, and emotionally stable. . . . The personal life of the scientist is thought to be quite shallow, his wife is not pretty, and his home is not very happy. He is rewarded by great personal satisfaction. . . . He enjoys moderate wealth and social status. . . . He is competent in organizing the world of things, but disdainful of the world of people . . . a masculine figure in a desexualized way.[1]

However, such studies omit one vital piece of information. They do not tell us precisely who it is that holds these views: whether, in this case, the stereotyped view of the scientist is shared by scientists themselves. Do they believe that their own personal lives are shallow; that their wives will not be pretty and

1. Beardslee and O'Dowd (1962).

their homes dull? If not, if the young scientists' view of science is a special one, we need to know how long it has been so. Did he reject the popular view of science before he chose science, or after? In short, we need specific information, more specific than the American research affords.

The Novelist and The Physicist

The method for the basic study was ready to hand: the *Semantic Differential*.[2] This is a questionnaire in which the individual rates a number of typical figures (in this case, 'Novelist', 'Historian', 'Mathematician', 'Physicist', etc.) against pairs of adjectives ('warm/cold', 'intelligent/stupid', 'hard/soft', 'valuable/worthless', and so on). He judges, for example, whether the Novelist is 'warm' or 'cold', and is free to use a 7-point scale expressing various degrees of emphasis – varying from 'extremely warm' to 'extremely cold'. He makes a large number of such judgements at considerable speed; and one trusts that he will be influenced more by intuition than by rational deliberation.[3]

Apparently, the myth of the scientist is one that Americans and English share.[4] Typical figures drawn from physical science, the Physicist for instance, were seen by the boys in my sample – consistently and overwhelmingly – as dependable, hard, hard-working, manly and valuable. Figures from the arts, such as the Novelist, were seen by contrast as imaginative, warm, exciting and smooth.[5]

2. Osgood *et al.* (1957).

3. In this first study, 30 typical figures were used, and 10 pairs of adjectives (each on a 7-point scale). In other words, each boy made 300 judgements. As the sample totalled 390, 117,000 judgements were made in all. The boys were drawn in approximately equal numbers from two schools (one grammar, one public), and fell into three age-groups: thirteen, fifteen and seventeen. Academically speaking, all of them were relatively bright.

4. I use the terms 'myth' and 'mythology' in a way which overlaps with anthropological usage, but is not identical to it. A 'myth' here is a belief or system of beliefs which although perhaps literally false, may none the less contain an element of meaning which is true in some more symbolic sense. Unlike most anthropologists, I do not restrict the term to beliefs expressed in the form of stories.

5. All differences mentioned here are statistically significant: the majority massively so. See Hudson (1967a).

It was obvious too that these myths influenced arts and physical science specialists alike. Admittedly, arts specialists thought that the Novelist and Physicist were equally intelligent, while the young scientists tended in this respect to favour the Physicist. But with every other quality, the judgements of the two groups about the Novelist and the Physicist were in agreement: both, for example, saw the Novelist as warm but undependable, the Physicist as dependable but cold. Arts and physical science specialists even agreed about the relative emphasis that should be placed on each of the adjectives. Both agreed that the characteristic most obviously differentiating the Novelist from the Physicist was his 'imaginativeness'; the quality differentiating him second most clearly was his 'warmth'; and so on.[6]

Some of the typical figures included in the *Semantic Differential* were women, and among them the Novelist's Wife, and the Research Scientist's Wife. Again results were consistent with those from America, and consistent from one group of specialists to another. Both arts and science specialists agreed that of the two, the Novelist's Wife was significantly the more exciting, feminine, soft, imaginative; whilst the Research Scientist's Wife was the more dependable. Agreement in the relative degree of emphasis placed on these adjectives was again high.[7]

The Artistic/Scientific Spectrum

Glancing down the results from the *Semantic Differential* one is struck by the tendency for certain typical figures to cluster together: Mathematician, Physicist, and Engineer clearly resemble each other closely in schoolboys' minds; and so too do Poet, Artist and Novelist. Examined in detail, this 'scientific' cluster can be broken down a little. The Engineer is seen as less intelligent, cold and dull than the other two, but as more manly, and dependable and imaginative. The Mathematician is seen as

6. This agreement is too high to express in terms of sorts and missorts. A more appropriate statistic is the rank order correlation coefficient: $r_S = 0.88$, $P < 0.01$, $n = 142$.

7. $r_S = 0.91$, $P < 0.01$.

even colder, duller and less imaginative than the Physicist.[8] At the other extreme, the Poet is seen as more intelligent than the Artist, but less warm and exciting; the Novelist is more imaginative and socially valuable than the Artist, but less soft and feminine. But these differences are all relatively small. When compared with other figures, both the scientific cluster and the artistic one are tight-knit.[9]

If these two clusters – the scientific and the artistic – are set up as polar opposites, the other professions represented form a spectrum between them. And the position of each profession on this spectrum reflects in certain ways what is known of their members from earlier research.

Nearest the scientific end of the spectrum is the Barrister; his scientific qualities easily outweighing his artistic ones. He is seen as highly intelligent, dull, hard, manly, dependable, hard-working; but as imaginative, and lacking in value. This fits well with the impression that law, at the university level, is attractive to the minority of arts specialists who are convergers.[10] It is certainly in keeping with the professional function of the solicitor, barrister, and judge, who work within an established system of legal principle and precedent. Near the mid-point of the scientific/ artistic spectrum, one finds the Biologist, with scientific and artistic qualities almost in balance. The Historian, likewise, presents a rather poorly differentiated picture. He is given the artistic qualities of relatively low intelligence, imaginativeness, warmth, smoothness and low value; but, to counterbalance these, he is seen as dull, manly and hard-working. Lastly the Psychologist: he presents a markedly artistic profile – imaginative, exciting, smooth, relatively lazy and relatively low in value. His scientific virtue is seen to be his intelligence, almost as high as the Barrister's, higher than the Engineer's.

8. In these respects he rivals the Trade Unionist; in middle-class schoolboys' eyes the possessor of every vice.

9. There is little overlap with other intermediate figures (Barrister, Psychologist) and no overlap at all between one cluster and the other.

10. Hudson (1966a).

Attractiveness Versus Value

Evidently, schoolboys take a more sanguine view of some professions than of others. Without question, the Mathematician, Physicist and Engineer are seen as more valuable than members of other professions; their value, in fact, is their outstanding quality. Although none of the figures on the artistic/scientific spectrum is rated as worthless, three come perilously close.[11] With the exception of the Psychologist, who does not seem to count in schoolboys' eyes as a scientist, the scientific figures are rated as massively more valuable than those connected in any way with the arts.

Despite this condemnation, there are signs that it is the artistic figures who are seen as the more attractive. This impression can be quantified in a number of ways. Three will do. First, the profile of each profession can be compared with those for certain other figures in the *Semantic Differential* which are defined as good: Good Father, Good Teacher, Good Friend. Second, each profile can be matched against a figure used in another version of the *Semantic Differential*: Ideal Self. Third, boys' usages of various value-loaded adjectives in the *Semantic Differential* can be intercorrelated.

Using the first method, the profiles for Good Father, Good Teacher and Good Friend were combined to form a composite creature – 'Good Male'. The professions showing the best match with Good Male were Novelist, Psychologist and Engineer. Barrister, Artist and Poet fell towards the middle of the field; while Physicist, Historian, Biologist and Mathematician brought up the rear. In other words, the connexion with boys' ratings of the value of these professions is inverse. Figures rated high for value tend to be rated low on their resemblance to Good Male.[12]

The second method depends on a test discussed in detail in

11. The Mathematician gains 73 per cent of the maximum rating possible on this quality, and the Physicist and Engineer are close behind. The Biologist comes next in value, just breaking 50 per cent; then follow Barrister (39 per cent), Novelist (31 per cent), Psychologist (25 per cent), Historian (9 per cent), Artist (7 per cent), Poet (4 per cent).

12. $r_S = -0.29$, $P > 0.05$.

Chapter 6. It turns out that apart from valuable, six adjectives are awarded by all boys to Ideal Self, and thus emerge as unambiguous virtues: warm, exciting and imaginative, manly, dependable and intelligent. The rating of each profession on these six virtues can be compared. The order, overall, agrees closely with that derived from Good Male, and, again, it is inversely related to ratings of value: Novelist, Barrister, Poet, Psychologist, Engineer, Artist, Historian, Physicist, Biologist, Mathematician.[13] The Novelist does well both times, and so too do the Barrister, Psychologist and Engineer. The Mathematician comes bottom twice running; the Biologist does poorly; and so do the Physicist and Historian.

This distinction between value and attractiveness is borne out by the analysis of correlations between adjectives.[14] A high correlation between two adjectives – manly and hard, say – would suggest that boys see their meanings as closely connected, using them virtually as synonyms; a low correlation indicates that boys see their meanings as clearly different; a negative correlation that the adjectives are opposed. In practice, certain adjectives intercorrelate highly, others not at all. There proved to be substantial positive correlations connecting the adjective valuable with dependable and intelligent.[15] But the correlations of valuable with the other four virtues – imaginative, exciting, warm, manly – were slight.[16]

All three methods, in other words, give clear evidence of a dissociation in boys' minds between what is valuable and what is appealing on more personal grounds. If such evidence has any bearing on the attractive power of university faculties, three predictions could be made. First, that the present swing from the scientific and towards the artistic end of the spectrum will continue.[17] Second, that engineering will tend to make ground

13. The relation between Ideal Self and Good Male estimates is high: $r_S = 0.85$, $P < 0.01$. The relation of the Ideal Self estimate to ratings of value is substantial and negative: $r_S = -0.50$, $P > 0.05$.

14. Based on usage over 20 typical figures. The method is described more fully in Chapter 5.

15. $r_S = 0.67$ and 0.59.

16. $r_S = 0.26$, 0.26, 0.23 and 0.03 respectively.

17. Dainton (1968). See also Chapter 9.

at the expense of the purer sciences.[18] Third, that the more humane branches of psychology will grow faster than the more biological.

Typical Graduates Questionnaire

An unmistakable implication of the data from the *Semantic Differential* is that adult scientists are seen as leading rather dull personal lives. It was with this in mind that a *Typical Graduates Questionnaire* was devised. Boys were asked to compare 'a typical arts graduate' and 'a typical science graduate' in the light of thirty characteristics, some general ('competitive with others'), others highly specific ('wears fashionable clothes').[19] A large proportion of these thirty characteristics yielded significant deviations in one direction or the other. Both arts and science specialists agreed that the arts graduate was more likely than the science graduate:

> to wear fashionable clothes. $(15 \cdot 01:1)$[20]
> to flirt with his secretary. $(9 \cdot 0:1)$
> to be sociable. $(6 \cdot 3:1)$
> to panic in emergencies. $(5 \cdot 8:1)$
> to like expensive restaurants. $(5 \cdot 3:1)$
> to gamble. $(4 \cdot 6:1)$
> to like his wife to look glamorous. $(4 \cdot 2:1)$
> to get into debt. $(4 \cdot 0:1)$
> to get divorced. $(2 \cdot 9:1)$

In contrast, the science graduate was seen by both groups as more likely than the arts graduate:

> to work long hours. $(14 \cdot 5:1)$
> to be faithful to his wife. $(4 \cdot 6:1)$
> to be competitive at work. $(2 \cdot 2:1)$
> to be embarrassed about sex. $(1 \cdot 7:1)$

18. Other studies have carried no hint of this. See, e.g. Hutchings (1963).

19. Responses were on a 5-point scale ranging from 'arts graduate much more likely' to 'science graduate much more likely'. The sample was of similar composition to the first: n=204, drawn from three schools – two public, one grammar.

20. These proportions are of sorts to missorts. In all instances, $P < 0 \cdot 05$. The agreement between the arts and physical science specialists in the rank ordering of items is again very high: for all 30 items in the questionnaire, $r_s = 0 \cdot 82$, $P < 0 \cdot 01$.

Whatever their speciality, the attitudes of boys towards the arts and sciences are clearly influenced by a common set of preconceptions. Both groups, arts and science specialists alike, see the typical arts graduate as the more pleasure-seeking and irresponsible figure, and the typical science graduate as the more puritanical.

The next step was to use the *Typical Graduates Questionnaire* on a much younger group: boys who were not only unspecialized, but who had had little or no exposure to science. A group of sixty new arrivals at a grammar school were chosen, fresh from the 11-Plus. Few had been taught much science, even at the humblest level, and several had difficulty with certain turns of phrase in the test itself.[21] The test, in other words, pressed quite close to the limits of their comprehension. Even so the beliefs existing among seventeen-year-olds were accurately reflected. Despite changes in detail, the broad outlines of the arts/science mythology were plain to see.[22] As before, the item most often taken to typify the arts graduate was 'wears fashionable clothes'; and that most typical of the science graduate, 'works long hours'. Although the stereotyping of perceptions was slightly less emphatic among the eleven-year-olds,[23] one was left with the suspicion that the mythology exists from the moment the concepts of 'arts' and 'science' are comprehensible; that concept and intuitive connotation reach the child's mind more or less simultaneously.[24]

The Identikit

Recently, I have approached these myths by two further routes. Both help to illuminate their nature and extent. The first depends

21. 'Prudish', for example, baffled a number.

22. Agreement in the rank ordering of items in the *Typical Graduates Questionnaire* for the eleven- and seventeen-year-old groups was high: $r_S = 0.72$, $P < 0.01$.

23. Between eleven and seventeen, certain items become more stereotyped: the arts man's tendency to 'like expensive restaurants', for example, 'to get divorced', 'to panic in emergencies'; and the scientist's tendency 'to be competitive with his workmates'. Others fade: the arts man's tendency to be 'a heavy smoker', and 'to help with the household chores'.

24. Relatively few major changes in stereotype occur between the ages of thirteen and seventeen. Those that do are discussed in Chapter 5.

on an 'identikit' procedure.[25] Each individual is invited to create four personalities, on the pretext that these are needed for a television play: two married couples – Mr and Mrs S, Mr and Mrs T. There are only three rules: that the personalities must be lifelike, distinguishable and constructed from the lists of qualities provided.[26] Each individual can construct whatever personalities he pleases – and marry them off as he sees fit. If stereotyped beliefs about personality influence the perception of the majority of people taking the *Identikit* Test, certain clusterings of qualities will be apparent in the results. If not, the results should be more or less random.

Results from the *Identikit* conform closely with those already described.[27] One attribute in the male list was 'Studied a science subject at university'. This was linked by boys, predictably enough, with other male attributes:

> interests are mechanical and technical. (4·8:1)
> cold. (3·7:1)
> manly. (2·5:1)
> unsociable. (2·2:1)
> dislikes talking about emotional, personal matters. (2·2:1)
> unimaginative. (2·1:1)
> happier dealing with things than with people. (1·9:1)[28]

It was also connected (as was each of the male attributes just listed) with the following attributes in the list for the wives:

> down to earth. (3·3:1)
> wears dowdy clothes. (3·2:1)
> has poor parents. (2·2:1)[29]

25. The idea is, I think, a new one.
26. Two lists of qualities are supplied, one applying to the husbands (Mr S and Mr T), the other to their wives (Mrs S and Mrs T). The qualities are presented in pairs of opposites. If one of the male qualities is given to Mr S, its opposite must be given to Mr T; and for their wives likewise. The *Identikit*'s only constraint lies in the selection and pairing of the qualities used; its only obvious inconvenience, the fact that the order of presentation may influence the stereotypes produced.
27. So far, used at only one school, boys aged fifteen to sixteen: n=53.
28. P=0·05 in each case.
29. Again, P <0·05 in each case. Conversely, the man who 'studied an arts subject at university' married the wife who is romantic, wears fashionable clothes, and has parents who are wealthy.

Arts Teacher and Science Teacher

The second line of attack was open-ended. The test defines two
men: Mr X, a teacher of physics and chemistry; and Mr Y, a
teacher of English literature and history. Boys were asked to jot
down in note form any thoughts which might cross the mind of
Mr X in the course of an ordinary working day; and then to
repeat the process for Mr Y. Initially, this caused some surprise.
Most schoolboys do not seem to realize spontaneously that their
teachers are people, nor that they have thoughts. As a result, a
number simply described the two men's behaviour. Others,
though, showed remarkable powers of impersonation, and what
their scripts reveal should by now be predictable enough.[30]

Eight qualities emerge as differentiating the Arts Teacher
(Mr Y) from the Science Teacher (Mr X). Of the two, the arts
teacher is seen as the more likely:

> to be sociable. (14·0:1)
> to reflect on his clumsiness and impracticality. (11·5:1)
> to communicate his material successfully. (6·7:1)
> to enjoy a sexual relationship with wife or girl friend. (5·7:1)
> to have sympathy for his students. (3·1:1)
> to be carefree rather than anxious. (2·8:1)
> to be satisfied with his job. (2·3:1)

Once again, there were no significant differences in the
perceptions of arts and physical science specialists. Throughout,
the master who teaches history and English is seen as the
happier, the more personable and the more libidinous of the two.
These views were produced by young men specializing respectively in physical science and classics:

Science Teacher (Mr X)
Good, Thursday only one period chemistry
Prefers Physics.
Damn, got to go by bus – car broken down.
O Hell there's that bore Mrs Jones up front don't want to talk to her.
Damn there's those little wretches in 3B to take 1st.

30. Tests used at three schools: n=151. Answers are bound to some extent to
reflect the idiosyncrasies of particular teachers. For this reason, a difference is
reported only if found at all three schools. In each case, $P < 0.05$.

Will these little morons never learn Archimedes.
O Good, now perhaps I can enjoy myself – VIB Physics
are so responsive and eager to learn.
Now Break suppose I've got to go and make polite small talk with those
up in the air arty people in the Common Room. Oh for a few more
people to talk Atomic physics with.
Why HM make me supervise lunch
Knows I hate it.
No afternoon school
Can go home to lab.
No afternoon school
Mary always disturbs me
– Coffee or tea dear
Why can't she leave me alone
Suppose I'd better go in to supper.
Damn her wanting to watch Z cars
there is the scientific programme on.
How nice my single bed
How can people sleep with their wives.

Arts Teacher (Mr Y)
How nice to travel train – plenty conversation.
Why no response to Lit. So enlightening.
Must be patient. No good forcing pace.
How I like Break – so chatty except X – Scientists indeed.
Coffee with cream–mm.
History they'll never learn.
Still got that headache.
Out to lunch. No one to talk to.
No afternoon lessons go to library to work.
4.30 home to see Jane
Shall be glad to see her.
Glad I've got such devoted wife.
Can't wait for supper.
Watch t.v. Good documentary.
To bed How nice to sleep with Jane.
Snuggle up.

Science Teacher (Mr X)
He gets up at eight o'clock. breakfast is usual fare – tea is badly made,
but he doesn't mind. He is thinking of what he is going to do. The
fifths are doing experiment – They won't find anything new. It will be

just as usual. The third year specialists are doing slightly more interesting work, but he's done it before, and they just sit there and mop it up. They're a clever lot, and he is proud of them. Mr Y goes off in a sports car, he thinks with envy. Then he goes home to lunch. His wife has cold lunch, with a musty taste. The room is decorated in bad taste; he doesn't mind. During the afternoon he corrects the papers. He sees a tree out of the window, thinks of the force in its roots. Supper is at seven o'clock and then he watches T.V.

Arts Teacher (Mr Y)
Mr Y is a young batchelor. As he gets up to make his breakfast he thinks of last night out with Jane, and looks forward to tonight. He read something about a new theory for Napoleon's defeat at Waterloo yesterday. He goes to school in the M.G. smiles at everyone pities Mr X. He likes the people in his History set. Talks to them for the first five minutes, then discusses the new theory. They're an interesting lot. Next he is doing Jane Austin, never heard anyone take that point of view before. He is learning. He discussed it with the others over coffee. Lunch is with Jane at the pub. After closing time he goes off to play tennis – see you at seven . . .

The experiment was repeated on a sample of eleven-year-olds, but proved rather beyond them. Even so, at least one script transmits the familiar message:

Science Teacher (Mr X)
Gets up about six takes his time getting up and thinks about what he is going to teach.

Arts Teacher (Mr Y)
Wakes up and layes in bed with his arm round his wife. Finally he gets up and makes a pot of tea. Walkes to school. He cracks jockes.

Sources of Myths

This evidence has an air of complete self-consistency. The myths about the arts and sciences exist; they possess both simple coherence and detailed elaboration; and everyone appears to share them. They are as much part of the common culture of schoolboys as syntax, schoolrooms, and football boots. It is arguable that such preconceptions are deplorable; that they embody precisely the arbitrariness and oversimplification of judgement that educational systems exist to expunge – idle prejudices fostered by the mass media in general, and television above all. If this also means that we should ignore them, I would disagree. In the first place, it is misleading to blame such preconceptions on popular journalism and television. These certainly present figures in stereotyped form. Probably, too, they help to fortify the myths which already exist in people's minds, and to undermine their critical capacity. But I cannot believe that the television's portrayal of the scientist, for instance, was invented at random. More likely is the view that entertainment is successful precisely to the extent that it can play upon the myths, assumptions and prejudices its audience already possesses.

A better explanation is one that interprets the myths of artist and scientist as personifications of the kind of work that artists and scientists are known to do. The novelist is known to describe human relations and experiences: he is fitted out with a personality to match – a talent for relationships and emotional sensitivity. The scientist specializes in ironmongery and cold logic: he is seen as cold, hard and impersonal. And so on. Even this can only be part of the story. We have more to explore and explain. What bearing have these myths on the actual state of novelists and scientists? Is the novelist really warm, the scientist dependable and cold? And what of the boys – large numbers of them each year – who choose careers in science believing as they do so that adult scientists have dull personal lives? Is their choice a reluctant compromise? Or is it made gladly, and with a sense of relief? And is it not possible that if scientists do indeed have dull lives and dowdy wives, they do so solely to act out what they perceive as society's expectations of them?

One is struck, too, by the evidence of the opposition in boys' minds between pleasure and value. The myth of the Artist is in many respects the embodiment, not so much of the work he does, as of the principle of irresponsible pleasure; that of the Scientist the embodiment of the protestant ideals of duty, responsibility and social value. This simple distinction seems in fact to carry others with it: the themes of Chapters 2 and 3 tend to recur. Masculinity seems to be seen by schoolboys as a minor puritan virtue, and femininity in men as a concomitant of pleasure. Also related are the ideas of self-expression and self-control; and, arguably, a respect for authority as well – or at least for behaviour (dependability, working long hours, faithfulness in matrimonial matters) that the authority of society deems correct.

This opposition of pleasure and value is itself heavy with historical connotation. The Choice of Hercules was a choice between a life of toil and glory, and one of ease and enjoyment. The opposition is built, too, into Freud's distinction of Id and Superego; one the source of irrational, pleasure-seeking impulses, the other the seat of conscience and self-control. Freud's distinction sprang in its turn from the popular psychology of his day, and from much of the moral philosophy that preceded him.[31] He himself viewed it as a model for the neuro-physiology of the brain. Although it is apparently of little use as such, it may yet have a bearing on our perceptions of our own minds' workings. Perhaps we are bound to see ourselves as for ever torn between the competing attractions of irresponsible desire and worthy self-control. Freud, the moral philosphers, and my schoolboys all seem to have drawn their preconceptions from a common stock: to have used the elementary paradigm of wilful child and controlling parent – or, more strictly, the wilful child's perception of parental control. What is intriguing is that the myths of the Artist and the Scientist should be tied so closely to so rudimentary and seemingly inappropriate a source.

31. Whyte (1962).

CHAPTER 5

DIFFERENCES IN PERCEPTION

To an extent that is remarkable, boys agree about the typical artist and the typical scientist. It is clear, too, that although the artist, the teacher of an arts subject, and the typical arts graduate are factually distinct, boys endow all three with a single personality. Similar elisions occur on the science side, embracing the physical scientist, the science teacher, and the typical science graduate. On the other hand, boys observe a clear division between physical and biological science, and see little or no connexion between either and psychology.

So far I have said almost nothing about individual differences in the perception of the common myth – except that large differences are the exception rather than the rule. They do exist, none the less, and are illuminating. Nor have I said much about boys' reactions to other figures in the *Semantic Differential*: Air Hostess, Nurse, Trade Unionist, Duke, Good Mother, Good Teacher, and so on. These were included precisely in the hope that responses might differ: that arts and physical science specialists might take a different view, for example, of figures such as the Air Hostess and Film Actress; and of figures from the immediate family circle – Good Mother, Good Father.

The analysis of this chapter all has the same aim: to detect signs that the arts/science mythology has some impact on the individuals who embrace it. To show that the myths are not an amusing artifact, floating free from the more down-to-earth processes of intellectual development and choice; rather, that they are an integral part of the framework within which such processes occur.

'Sharpeners' and 'Faders'

Of differences between arts specialists and scientists, some of the most interesting concern changes in perception that occur from one age level to another. Although the total amount of stereotyping found at the thirteen-, fifteen- and seventeen-year-old age levels is much the same, the consensus about certain figures fades over the four years between thirteen and seventeen, while with others it grows sharper.[1] Others still reach a peak of definition at the fifteen-year-old level and then fade; and others remain roughly steady over the whole four-year span.

An explanation of the 'faders' is not far to seek. It turns out that they are all typical figures included in the test as having some emotional or sexual significance: Good Father, Good Mother, Good Teacher, Film Actress, Air Hostess. Presumably, each year they grow older, adolescent boys are more detached from the figures of emotional significance in their lives, and perceive them more dispassionately. Hence the consensus among thirteen-year-olds that Air Hostess and Film Actress embody all the feminine virtues has, by the age of seventeen, begun to collapse. During the four-year interval, Film Actress crosses the frontier from intelligent to stupid, from imaginative to unimaginative, and drops from being exceptionally exciting to being only moderately so. Good Mother also drops sharply from being thought very exciting to being border-line dull. The special interest of the process of disenchantment lies in the fact that it is most pronounced among boys studying the arts.[2]

More puzzling is the relationship of 'sharpening', 'peaking' and remaining 'steady' to the position of figures on the artistic/scientific spectrum. All three artistic figures 'sharpen' (Poet, Novelist, Artist); all the figures from physical science remain 'steady' (Mathematician, Physicist, Engineer, Research Scientist); all four of those from the middle of the spectrum 'peak' at fifteen (Barrister, Biologist, Historian, Psychologist).[3] Why?

1. Of 300 *Semantic Differential* judgements made by each boy, 93 were most sharply stereotyped among thirteen-year-olds, 114 among fifteen-year-olds, and 93 among seventeen-year-olds.

2. 2·7:1. When modern linguists are excluded (see below), 4·2:1. P <0·001, n=136. The most sceptical group were the specialists in politics and economics; and like other arts boys, especially so about Good Father. Surprisingly, one group was consistently out of line: the modern linguists were easily the most indulgent of all. Differences between these and other arts specialists were often massive. Though odd, this is somewhat reminiscent of an earlier finding that modern linguists tend to be immature and uncommitted in their interests; Hudson (1966a).

3. The usual statistical tests seem inappropriate here; even so such a patterning cannot often arise by chance.

Clearly one makes little headway trying to interpret these changes in terms of the seventeen-year-old's greater knowledge of the world and the careers it contains. As far as one can tell, it is not true that stereotypes collapse as factual knowledge increases: if they did, all stereotypes would tend to 'fade'. Nor does it seem relevant that the seventeen-year-old has a greater command of language than the thirteen-year-old, and hence more skill in constructing mythical figures. If this were so, all stereotypes would 'sharpen'. I remain baffled and have only one speculation to offer. There is some evidence that young scientists commit themselves to science at a younger age than arts specialists commit themselves to the arts.[4] It may be that the growth of emotional involvement in artistic matters is a manifestation of middle and late adolescence, while scientific interests develop earlier; that aesthetic awareness is linked to sexual maturation, whereas an awareness of science is not.[5] Differences in the rate of development of artistic and scientific interests; differences in rate of sexual maturation; and boys' perceptions of the arts and sciences – all three may prove to be interlocked. In what ways, it would at present be idle to guess.

The Halo Effect

The rest of the evidence in this chapter is concerned in one way or another with the bias or partiality of boys' judgements. When asked to make judgements about such figures as the Novelist, the Physicist, and their respective Wives, it is not surprising that arts and science specialists reveal a certain amount of bias. Arts specialists tend to play down the weaknesses associated with the Novelist, while the science boys play down those attached to the figures from science. The size of these 'halo effects' can be estimated by comparing the judgements of interested parties with those of schoolboys as a whole.

4. Lunt (1967); Butler (1968).
5. American evidence indicates that young scientists may reach sexual maturity later than average. Roe (1953) reports, for instance, that young scientists are typically not very interested in girls, date for the first time late in college, marry the first girl they date, and thereafter appear to show a rather low level of heterosexual drive.

There are two important facts about the halo effects in the present data. The first is that although some haloes are large, they clearly overlay the generally accepted myths about the arts and sciences rather than disrupting them.[6] Second, the size of the haloes differs greatly from one group (and one typical figure) to another. The proportion of the judgements made about the Novelist, the Novelist's Wife, the Physicist, and Research Scientist's Wife that can be attributed to halo effect are 25·2 per cent, 19·3 per cent, 34·5 per cent and 7·6 per cent respectively. In three cases out of four, in other words, the halo is substantial; and it is especially marked in young physical scientists' assessments of the Physicist. Even so, there are occasions on which interested parties are not over-generous but unduly modest. This is most marked in the physical scientists' view of the Research Scientist's Wife: they see her as less imaginative and cultured, and more unhappy than do boys as a whole.[7]

The evidence indicates, in other words, that boys' loyalty to their own group imposes a systematic bias on their perception; and that in their expression of this bias arts specialists and young scientists reveal a difference in their attitude to women. The second of these findings harks back to Chapter 3, and to the theme of masculine identification. It seems that young scientists are specially prone to inflate the merits of the (presumably male) Physicist, whilst having no special investment in the Research Scientist's Wife. The equivalent distinction in the arts specialists' judgements is by comparison slight.[8] This confirms the impression that the young scientist lives in a man's world where the importance of women is marginal. By contrast, the qualities of a wife seem – in the young arts specialists' eyes – almost as

6. See Hudson (1967a). The relevant statistic is the rank order correlation co-efficient. In practice, each group tends to be generous to their own figure; but the ordering of adjectives is remarkably similar in each case: $r_s = 0·88$, P $< 0·01$, for the comparison between Novelist and Physicist; $r_s = 0·91$, P $< 0·01$, for that between Novelist's Wife and Research Scientist's Wife.

7. Generally, arts boys tend to claim scientific virtues for the Novelist (intelligent and valuable), rather than to boost up the artistic values he is generally thought to possess. With science boys the reverse is true. The qualities that account for the halo around the Physicist are the artistic virtues; warm, imaginative, and exciting.

8. The difference in size of these two halo effects, expressed as a proportion is $2·5:1$. P $< 0·001$ n=142.

important to a man's self-esteem as the qualities he possesses himself.

Clusters of Adjectives

I want to shift now from the typical figures in the *Semantic Differential*, to the adjectives: to the use that arts and physical science specialists make of language. Here arts/science differences are substantial, and their implications absorbing. Although superficially unrelated to the halo effect, the two sets of data prove to have much in common.

The *Semantic Differential* seems a superficial and fakeable technique, but when analysed in terms of adjectival clusters rather than of typical figures, it lays bare boys' assumptions and values in ways which they would find it hard to disguise. The less two adjectives are discriminated in boys' minds, the higher the correlation between those two adjectives – the closer the linkage, the tighter the cluster. The more clearly the meanings of two adjectives are distinguished, the lower the correlation, the looser the cluster.

Looking at the responses of boys as a whole, one sees that the artistic virtues (warm, exciting and imaginative) cluster together quite closely; and to a lesser extent, the scientific virtues (valuable, dependable and intelligent) do likewise. The connexions between these two clusters are more slender.[9] In addition, there is a third cluster: manly, hard, rough – as opposed to feminine, soft, smooth.[10] At its masculine pole, this third cluster is linked to the scientific virtues; and at its feminine pole to the artistic ones.[11]

The real interest of these adjectival clusters lies, however, in the differences between arts specialists and physical scientists. The connexions just quoted in fact conceal large differences in linguistic habit between one group and the other. Each group

9. Correlations between adjectives based on 20 typical figures. Those linking warm, exciting and imaginative: $r_S = 0.73$, 0.73, 0.81. Those linking valuable, dependable, intelligent: $r_S = 0.36$, 0.59, 0.67. Those linking warm. exciting and imaginative with valuable, dependable and intelligent: $r_S = 0.08 - 0.42$; median $r_S = 0.24$.

10. These three adjectives, again, cluster quite closely: $r_S = 0.62$, 0.72, 0.78.

11. In the first case, $r_S = 0.23 - 0.59$; in the second, $r_S = 0.12 - 0.65$.

clusters adjectives after its own fashion. Physical scientists, for example, see a positive connexion between manly and valuable, whereas among arts boys the connexion runs the other way: they associate valuable not with manly but with feminine. The same is true of the connexion between manly and intelligent. In fact a high proportion of the differences between the usages of the arts and physical science specialists are statistically significant.[12]

I had stared at these differences for several weeks before they fell into a coherent pattern. It could scarcely have been more simple: boys cluster together the adjectives that apply to their own group. The adjectives linked more closely by the arts boys than by the physical scientists are the artistic virtues (warm, imaginative and exciting), and the feminine qualities (smooth, soft and feminine). Those linked more closely by the scientists are the scientific virtues (valuable, dependable, intelligent), and the masculine qualities (rough, hard and manly). This tendency is almost perfectly consistent. Of twenty-five relevant inter-correlations, twenty-one conform and there are only four marginal exceptions. The result, in other words, is analogous to the halo effect; loyalty to a group blurs the individual's capacity for dispassionate judgement. Also reminiscent of the halo effect is the fact that the masculinity/femininity cluster is tighter knit in the responses of physical scientists than it is in those of arts boys: it is the scientists who seem to have a simpler, less differentiated idea of sexual identity than do the arts specialists.[13] But despite the broad similarity between this evidence and that from the halo effect, the results are now more complex and their implications more subtle. The finding is worth considering with some care.

12. Hudson (1967b). Of 36 connexions between the nine adjectives quoted above, 15 show significant differences between arts specialists and physical scientists: in six cases, $P < 0.001$; in three $P < 0.01$; in six $P < 0.05$, $n = 142$. Initially, intercorrelations were calculated by rank order correlation (r_S). Though quick, this is wasteful of data, and cannot be used to test the significance of differences between correlations. So the whole operation was repeated, each boy's use of each adjective being punched, and related as simple matching coefficients. See Sokal and Sneath (1963). Happily, the results differed only in detail from the first approximation.

13. For science boys, the correlations between manly, hard and rough are: $r_S = 0.73$, 0.78, 0.82; for arts boys: 0.52, 0.62, 0.79. Two of these three represent significant differences: $P < 0.01$.

Discrimination and a Sense of Belonging

Boys, it seems, tend to cluster together – that is to say, they tend to use without discrimination – those adjectives that they know are normally applied to members of their own speciality. In some respects this is a remarkable finding. It seems to contradict the principle that our discrimination of an object gets sharper, the more familiar with that object we become; the principle that, to the Chinaman, all Occidentals look alike. Like most psychological generalities, this one clearly deserves a second look. In some sphere, aesthetic discrimination for example, the principle seems to work well. Only years of practice would enable us to tell Chelsea from Bow, Crespi from Piazzetta, Worth from Dior. The same is true of our social perceptions: we are prone to lump unfamiliar groups together – and to see evil in them.[14] But in the sphere of language, it seems, this tendency is reversed. The adjectives we apply to ourselves we tend to scramble together and treat as synonymous; those we apply to others we differentiate more clearly. It is as though one side-effect of group membership were to cloud our capacity for verbal discrimination. This clouding affects not only our judgements about ourselves, but our general use of those adjectives which typify our group.[15]

In fact, this finding is not so much at odds with everyday experience as one might think. Students of infant behaviour have sometimes remarked that young children tend to take those close to them for granted – their mothers especially; and there is also some evidence that successful marriages depend on the fantasies of the two people concerned rather than on their capacity for dispassionate perception of one another.[16] The implication is that there is a pale of emotional intimacy within which the capacity for objective discrimination fails; that there is some feature of close emotional relationships which renders

14. See Adorno *et al.* (1950).
15. There are parallels here with work on 'reference groups'. See Jones and Gerard (1967) for a summary.
16. Corsini (1956). His finding is that successful marriages are those in which both husband and wife see the husband's sex role in highly stereotyped terms. The wife's sex role is apparently irrelevant. A number of other studies support this; Dornbusch (1967).

detached judgement impossible. My own finding about adjectival clusters suggests that our occupational group or profession
falls within this pale rather than outside it; and that our sense of
belonging influences our judgement – even when thinking about
topics which are ostensibly unrelated to us.

What happens, we may ask, when the figures under consideration do have a close and an immediate relevance to ourselves?
Granted that the arts boy tends to cluster artistic qualities when
he is making judgement about a wide range of figures (the Army
Officer and the Athlete, as well as the Engineer and the Poet);
what happens when we look specifically at his reactions to the
arts figures: Novelist, Poet, Historian, and Artist? Is his lack of
discrimination particularly marked when he is nearest to home?
On the strength of the analogy with the halo effect, one would
expect this to be so. Likewise with young physical scientists.
When judging the Mathematician, Physicist, Engineer, and
Research Scientist, does he cluster the scientific qualities even
more closely than before?

Fortunately for my argument, this is exactly what happens.
When the analysis is restricted to the four arts figures, the
tendency of arts boys to assimilate the artistic qualities into one
cluster is greatly increased. They not only assimilate the artistic
qualities; they tend to pre-empt some of the scientific virtues as
well: valuable and intelligent, and to a lesser extent manly and
dependable. When judging arts figures, the science boys' use of
adjectives is much the more discriminative.[17] In judging the
scientific figures, exactly the reverse occurs. It is the science
boys who lack discrimination, and the arts boys who use adjectives with the more finesse.[18]

The Relevance of the Myths

Taken together, Chapters 4 and 5 tell against the view that the
myths are a trivial affair. They suggest instead that in his choice
between the arts and sciences, the intelligent boy aligns himself

17. 21 out of 36 correlations show significant differences between arts and physical
science specialists: in 16, scientists' discrimination is greater than arts specialists';in
5, vice versa. In each case, P <0·05.

18. 16 out of 36 correlations show significant differences: in 13, arts boys are more
discriminative than the young scientists; in 3 vice versa. P <0·05.

intuitively on a number of psychic dimensions: respect for conventional values, for example; masculinity; and pleasure-seeking as opposed to self-control. Such simple polarities are not the whole of human experience, nor are they wholly simple. Other more material factors play their part: mental endowment, the pressures of school and family, economic opportunity. But these polar oppositions do seem to represent the context, the frame of reference, within which the individual's sense of his own identity evolves. And once a choice of career is made, and the foundations of a working identity laid, it seems likely that the individual's perception of the common myths begins to change. A man chooses to become a scientist because he finds the prospect of science comfortable; but once a scientist, he begins to see the world from the scientist's point of view.

The evidence from the halo effect also shows that boys, arts specialists and scientists alike, view the mythical attributes of their chosen profession with a certain defensiveness. They feel uneasy about the faults. This quality of defensiveness is not one that is easily expressed in a statistic; it is clear enough though in the writings of adults. The two examples I have chosen are from science. This is not because scientists have a monopoly of this quality,[19] but because among scientists its expression is often undisguised.

Consider the songs that the physicists of the Cavendish Laboratory used to sing to themselves at parties in the earlier and palmier days of this century – the days of Rutherford and J. J. Thomson:

Air: 'Solomon Levi'.
>   My name is J. J. Thomson and my lab's in
>   Free School Lane,
>   If once a man has been inside he's sure to
>   come again,
>   Here some do play with Töpler pumps, and
>   some with liquid air,
>   And some do play the giddy goat, but
>   that's not here nor there.

19. No one exposed, for instance, to the tawdry preciosity of Bloomsbury could think this for a moment.

Chorus: Oh! J. J. Thomson, J. J. Tra-la-la-la.
           Sir Joseph Thomson, Tra-la-la-la-la-la
             la-la-la-la-la,

           My name is J. J. Thomson, and my lab's
             in Free School Lane,
           There's no professor like J. J. my students
             all maintain,
           I've been here six-and-twenty-years, and
             here I shall remain,
           For all the boys just worship me at my
             lab in Free School Lane.

           The people are delighted with the wondrous
             things we do,
           But few have any notion that we're such a
             jolly crew,
           If some of them were here tonight I think
             we'd make it plain
           We're not all just as dry as dust at the lab
             in Free School Lane![20]

The implication of these awesome ditties – 'Ions Mine' is
another – is of some personal impoverishment in the scientist.
The singers seem eager to convince us, perhaps themselves, that
this is apparent not real; that they are indeed a jolly crew, and
that a jolly crew is a good thing to be.

Over the last half century, manners have changed and scientific wit has become crisper. All the more surprising therefore to
find the same sense of unease permeating a more recent product
of the Cavendish: Watson's memorable account of the discovery
of the structure of DNA.[21] The author intersperses his descriptions of the discovery itself and his comments about his friends
and rivals, with information about his social life as a young
American post-doctoral student, for the most part in Cambridge:

Kalckar, however, was obviously cultivated, and Luria hoped that in
his civilized, continental company I would learn the necessary tools to
do chemical research, without needing to react against the profit-
oriented organic chemists. (p. 22)

20. Thomson (1964), p. 98.
21. Watson (1968): required reading for anyone interested in science or scientists.

... Kendrew made a favorable impression on Luria; like Kalckar, he was civilized and in addition supported the Labor Party. (p. 39)

... dinner was often gay, especially after the wine turned the conversation to the currently talked-about Cambridge popsies. (p. 65)

... for relief, Maurice had taken up interference microscopy to find a trick for weighing chromosomes. (p. 148)

... her X-ray pictures were getting prettier and prettier. (p. 148)

Also living at Pop's was Bertrand Fourcade, the most beautiful male, if not person, in Cambridge.... Odile was admiring Bertrand's perfectly proportioned face as he spoke of his problems choosing among potential social engagements during his forthcoming summer on the Riviera. (pp. 173-4)

... Peter held forth on how Lord Rothschild was avoiding his responsibility as a father by not inviting him to dinner with his daughter Sarah. (p. 176)

... after tea I would show up for only a few minutes of minor fiddling before dashing away to have sherry with the girls at Pop's. (p. 180)

... unless some very special trick existed, randomly twisting two polynucleotide chains around one another should result in a mess. (p. 182)

Both were genuinely pleased, Elizabeth with sisterly pride, Bertrand with the idea that he could report back to International Society that he had a friend who would win a Nobel Prize. (p. 199)

Odile looked in horror at the prospect of being long without fashionably dressed people. (p. 203)

Item by item, the author ticks off the faults of the stereotypical scientist – dull, excessively hard-working, uninterested in sex, lower class. He tells us that, although a scientist, he is urbane and a little lazy, that his interest in sex is forthright, and that if he is not aristocratic at least his company is welcome to those who are. His style too is consciously light: he uses words like 'game', 'gimmick', and 'trick' repeatedly, and 'pretty' both of science and of girls. The reader is left convinced only that there is an image of the scientist that this brilliantly gifted man feels driven to disown. Although engagingly wry, his claim for himself is less modest: he wants to be seen to combine the virtues of both arts and science, and to harbour the faults of neither. This impulse is the subject of the first experiment in the chapter which follows.

CHAPTER 6

THE PERCEPTION OF SELF

HIDDEN beneath the relatively smooth surface of the last two chapters, there still lurks an awkward and potentially dangerous finding. Though boys show few inhibitions in reproducing the stereotyped view of their own academic group, they seem unwilling – as was Professor Watson – to take the logical step, and apply these stereotypes directly to themselves. Of the thirty figures included in the original *Semantic Differential*, one was Self. In response, boys produced not the profile of their own speciality, but a catalogue of pure virtue. For arts and science boys alike, the resemblance between Self and that composite paragon Good Male was exceedingly close. Irrespective of their subject, all boys claimed to be warm, imaginative, exciting, manly, dependable, intelligent and valuable. In the cases of dependable and valuable, modesty overtook them a little; here they rated themselves lower than Good Male. But they equalled Good Male in intelligence, and gave themselves even higher ratings for manliness.[1] Indeed, the Self of the young physical scientists was nearly as close to their view of the Novelist as it was to their view of the Physicist, good qualities being pilfered from the artistic and scientific ends of the spectrum with equal aplomb.[2]

This finding is dangerous, for if the notion of 'self' is so completely divorced from that of the group or profession to which the individual belongs, critics might argue that the mythology of the arts and sciences (and of professions generally)

1. This hint of over-compensation supports the view that sexual identity is a topic on which English schoolboys are touchy. This may help to explain the disappointing results towards the end of Chapter 3.
2. The logic of such human frailty is familiar enough: all psychologists are emotionally disturbed; I am a psychologist; I am not emotionally disturbed. All businessmen are philistines; I am a businessman; appearances to the contrary, I am sensitive to higher things. The argument applies to all professions and all forms of disapprobation.

is irrelevant to any choice of career the individual makes. And if this is so, the study of boys' perceptions of the arts and sciences is a waste of time. Consequently, I set myself the task of forcing the Selves of arts and science boys apart; of demonstrating that the mythology has a direct influence on the self-perceptions of the boys concerned. This chapter deals, then, with a crucial link: the connexion between the individual's idea of himself and the behaviour he is willing and able to display. More generally, it leads to questions of self-awareness and candour: the extent to which convergers realize that they are convergers, and divergers that they are divergers; and the processes whereby the individual constructs his idea of who he is. At first sight, these problems may seem a little wispy, dealing in the philosophical rather than practical. Yet the issue is a basic one – both to my book and to my subject. For if connexions cannot be found between an individual's perceptions of his culture, his profession and his colleagues on the one hand, and his perception of himself on the other, my research lies broken-backed. I should be left with unrelated fragments: pieces about myths and stereotypes, pieces about individual differences in ability and personality – all of which look interesting in themselves, but whose connexions, as so often in psychology, can only be guessed at.

The Four Selves

The difficulty with the *Semantic Differential* Self led to an experiment which gives me a certain pleasure. This work was based on a technique the potentialities of which I have only just begun to explore.[3] It seemed possible that if questions were more clearly defined, the Self described by an arts specialist might come to resemble the Novelist, while the Self offered by the young physical scientist might resemble the Physicist. In all probability large haloes of self-approbation were unavoidable; but my hope was that their glow could be reduced sufficiently for the outlines of a more dispassionate perception to show through. If young physicists could admit that the Physicist had

3. The method has affinities with Kelly's (1955) work on repertory grids and Laing *et al.* (1966) on interpersonal perception.

certain faults, I wanted them to admit that they had the same faults themselves; likewise with the young arts specialists. If the mythology could be shown to influence boys' perception of themselves, this would be evidence in favour of the view that the mythology influences career choice. If not, the evidence of the last two chapters could still be seen as academic.

Rather than slipping Self in as one of an assortment of otherwise more objective figures, I asked boys to distinguish between certain aspects of Self. Using the *Semantic Differential* format, they were asked to describe:

Actual Self (who they actually were).
Ideal Self (who they would like to be).
Perceived Self (who their teachers took them to be).
Future Self (who they expected to be in, say, 10 years time).

In the original *Semantic Differential* they were urged to respond quickly, off the cuff; now I asked them to take especial care. I also stressed the need for frankness. Otherwise the method was as before, each of the four Selves being rated in the light of the familiar adjectives.

The results were gratifying. The Selves of arts boys and physical scientists separated themselves out in just the way I had hoped. The halo effects surrounding the Selves were substantially reduced – in some cases by well over a half – and the common view of the Arts Man and the Scientist began to show through. Arts boys admitted that although warm, imaginative and exciting, they were somewhat lacking in manliness, dependability and value; and likewise the scientists owned up to the faults of their profession – to being relatively cold, dull, and unimaginative.

However, the amount of shift varied greatly, depending on which of the four Selves was in question: Actual, Ideal, Perceived, Future. These variations give the results from the *Four Selves* a curious twist. With the artistic virtues (imaginative, warm and exciting) the best differentiation between the Selves of the arts and physical science specialists was produced by Actual Self. The scientific virtues, on the other hand (valuable, dependable, intelligent, and manly) were discriminated best by

Perceived Self.[4] Further, the two pairs of adjectives in the *Semantic Differential* which do not have a clear value loading – hard/soft, rough/smooth – were differentiated best neither by Actual nor by Perceived Self, but by Ideal Self.[5]

In other words, it is Actual Self which enables boys to be detached about their possession of artistic virtues, and Perceived Self about their possession of scientific ones.[6] A tempting inference is that artistic virtues are perceived accurately by internal reference, by looking inside oneself; while scientific virtues are perceived accurately by reference to the reactions of others – and especially to figures of authority, like the teacher. This concurs neatly with the psychoanalytic view that artistic virtues are essentially 'libidinous', and spring from within, whereas the scientific qualities are those acquired (like the conscience or 'super ego') by adopting as our own the opinions of some frightening figure external to us.[7] Interpretative difficulties notwithstanding, there is clearly a distinction in boys' minds about the nature of the artistic and scientific virtues; one set of virtues being *seen* to spring from within, the other as vested in external authority. It is the notion of who one really is that encourages a dispassionate acceptance of the myth as far as the artistic virtues are concerned; while the notion of what one's teachers think elicits this for the virtues associated with science.

If this interpretation is approximately correct, it seems to follow that arts specialists identify themselves as people whose cardinal virtues spring from the freedom of their emotional lives,

4. There is one exception and this only marginal: 'intelligent'. This was differentiated slightly better by Future Self.

5. If a composite profile is produced using Actual Self for the artistic virtues, Perceived Self for the scientific virtues and Ideal Self for the more neutral qualities, the Selves of arts and science boys can then be matched against the general consensus for Novelist and Physicist. Plots of Self were found to have moved on average 52 per cent of the distance from the original, totally 'haloed' position towards the consensus. This movement is reasonably consistent adjective by adjective, ranging from 34 per cent for valuable to 78 per cent for smooth.

6. This is overwhelmingly the case with 'exciting'; solidly so for 'imaginative', 'manly' and 'dependable'; marginally so with 'warm', 'intelligent' and 'valuable'. The discrimination overall is highly significant, $3.5:1$, $P < 0.001$, $n = 79$.

7. See, e.g. Erikson (1963), Sears *et al.* (1966).

and whose faults arise from a failure or unwillingness to heed external authority. Young scientists, on the other hand, appear to identify themselves as people whose virtues spring from without, and whose faults arise from their failure or unwilling-ness to allow their emotions sufficient rein.[8]

Future Self

The *Four Selves* technique permits other types of analysis, only one or two of which have so far been explored. The test, for example, can be scored for discrepancies between Selves. The results of the last few pages imply that these should differentiate convergers from divergers. Scores are available so far only from one school. Even so, consistent differences emerge, and in one case at a highly significant level. Convergers seem less likely than divergers to differentiate between Actual and Ideal Self; between Perceived and Future Self; and between Actual and Future Self.[9] Overall, divergers are almost exactly twice as likely as convergers to differentiate between the various Selves; but easily the largest of these differences is that between Actual and Future Self. This suggests that by the age of fifteen or sixteen, con-vergers are much more settled than divergers about the kind of person they expect to become. It may well be that sublects like physical science hold a strong attraction for boys who envisage relatively little change in their own character and way of life.[10] If the proportion of boys unwilling to commit themselves at an early age to a career and a settled view of their own future is

8. This distinction has parallels in sociological grand theory. Parsons and Shils (1951), for example, envisage human action as arising from the interplay of role expectations vested in institutions, and the personality and predispositions of the individual. My evidence is phenomenological not sociological – it deals with boys' perceptions of institutions and of themselves, not with boys and institutions as they 'actually' are. It may not be without interest to sociologists, even so.

9. 2·2:1, 3·7:1 and 14·0:1, $P < 0.05$, < 0.05 and < 0.001, respectively.

10. This inference is supported by Lunt's evidence, quoted in Chapter 5, that young scientists tend to commit themselves to science at an earlier age than arts specialists choose the arts. It is interesting, too, that the present small sample of convergent arts specialists appear to have different self-perceptions from convergent scientists. This work will have to be repeated, though, on a more adequate sample.

increasing, this in itself might well explain the current swing away from physical science at the sixth-form level and at university.[11]

Mr A and Mr B

These data lead to the more general question of the insight that boys have into their own temperament and mental powers. Do convergers know that they are convergers, and divergers that they are divergers? I used two approaches to this question, both naïve. First, convergers and divergers were presented with brief, highly stereotyped descriptions of two men – Mr A and Mr B – and asked which of the two they more closely resembled. Mr A was described as follows:

Enjoys precise logical argument.
Dislikes discussion of personal, emotional matters.
Hobbies are practical and mechanical.
Happier dealing with things than with people.

Mr B is the antithesis:

Dislikes precise logical argument.
Enjoys discussion of personal, emotional matters.
Hobbies are literary and artistic.
Happier dealing with people than with things.

By rights, most convergers should choose to identify themselves with Mr A, and most divergers with Mr B. In practice they do so.[12]

When put in the form of a choice between alternatives, boys almost always identified Mr A as the science graduate, and Mr B as the arts graduate. Further, boys specializing in physical science showed a strong tendency to identify themselves with Mr A, and boys specializing in the arts, with Mr B.[13] Mr A and

11. Dainton (1968). See, too, Chapter 9. The 'Swing from Science' may also be seen as a retreat from the puritanical connotations of science. For a study of resistance to change among students, see Johnson Abercrombie (1960).

12. The situation is complicated by the fact that Mr B turned out to be a more attractive figure than Mr A. Even so, the discrimination works well, $3 \cdot 1:1$, $P < 0 \cdot 01$, $n = 46$. Tested at one school only.

13. $6 \cdot 9:1$, $P < 0 \cdot 001$, $n = 125$.

Mr B were laden by all boys alike with the stereotypes already associated with the arts and the sciences. When asked to say which six from a list of twelve adjectives his friends would use in describing Mr A, an overwhelming majority picked out cold, and large majorities chose hard, intelligent, rough, manly and dependable.[14] The adjectives selected for Mr B were – overwhelmingly – warm, and also imaginative, exciting, smooth, soft and undependable.[15]

The test also gave one the opportunity to measure the extent to which boys were thinking in stereotyped terms. Of the boys who identify themselves with Mr A – that is, as convergers – almost exactly three-quarters attributed the twelve adjectives in close or perfect accord with the cultural myths about the arts and sciences; of those who identified themselves with Mr B, only just over half did so.[16] Equivalent differences were found between actual convergers and divergers; and also between arts specialists and physical scientists. In other words, convergers, boys who identify themselves as convergers, and physical science specialists all tend to accept the cultural myths of the arts and sciences unquestioningly. Among divergers, boys who describe themselves as divergers, and arts specialists, this acceptance is only partial.

Perception of Ability

The second line of approach was even more literal-minded than the first. An IQ test and an open-ended test were given to three groups of boys.[17] These three groups were in fact the top three streams of a public school fifth form. Having completed the testing, I explained the scoring system to the boys and asked them (a) how well they thought they had done on the two types of test, and (b) which of their form-mates would have done well on them.

Superficially dull, the results are in one or two respects

14. Ranging from 124·0:1 to 2·1:1, $P < 0·05$.
15. Ranging from 124·0:1 to 1·4:1, $P < 0·05$.
16. 1·3:1, $P < 0.025$.
17. Part I of A. H. 5 and *Uses of Objects*; $n = 73$.

remarkable. Immediately apparent was a strong connexion, far stronger than I had found among older boys, between IQ and academic accomplishment. The school is one which not only streams by ability, but publishes a School List in which each boy's position reflects his examination results. Five of the seven boys with the highest IQs were in the top third of the top stream; six of the seven with the lowest IQs were in the bottom of the three streams.[18] On the other hand, the relation of the open-ended test to academic ability was effectively nil.[19] The relation of IQ to open-ended scores was zero, precisely. It followed that when open-ended and IQ scores were combined to give a convergence/divergence score, the convergers were more than twice as likely as the divergers to be academically successful.[20]

When self-estimates and form-mates' estimates were compared to reality, all were found to correlate positively. On the whole, self-estimates were more accurate than those of form-mates; estimates of IQ were consistently more accurate than those of open-ended scores; and divergers were significantly more accurate than convergers in guessing what their actual abilities might be.[21]

Apart from the greater accuracy of the divergers' self-perception, the results so far were reassuring but rather dull. More interesting was the degree of trust that boys placed in the School List when estimating each other's IQs. Even though the test was described throughout as the 'one right answer test', boys high on the List were automatically assumed to have high IQs, while boys low on it were assumed to have low ones.[22] The

18. $4 \cdot 0 : 1$, $P < 0 \cdot 001$, $n = 73$.

19. Actually, it was slightly negative, $1 : 1 \cdot 1$.

20. $2 \cdot 3 : 1$, $P < 0 \cdot 01$. Getzels and Jackson (1962) found convergers and divergers more or less equally successful in American High Schools. The difference is probably due to the fiercely competitive nature of English secondary education.

21. Self-estimates $v.$ actual IQ, $5 \cdot 7 : 1$; form-mates' estimates $v.$ actual IQ, $3 \cdot 2 : 1$. Equivalent proportions for the open-ended test, $2 \cdot 2 : 1$ and $1 \cdot 4 : 1$ respectively. Accuracy of divergers' self-estimates $v.$ accuracy of convergers', $2 \cdot 5 : 1$, $P < 0 \cdot 025$. There were also clear tendencies for boys who were actually convergers to find the IQ test both easier to do than the open-ended one, and more enjoyable.

22. $19 \cdot 5 : 1$, $P < 0 \cdot 001$. This of course is a far stronger connexion than the actual relation between IQ and the List ($4 \cdot 0 : 1$) would warrant.

influence of the List on form-mates' estimates of open-ended scores was positive but much smaller.[23] And it is interesting to see that while boys in the top stream were much the most accurate at guessing each other's IQs, they were the least accurate in estimating each other's open-ended scores.[24]

It seems, in other words, that in a highly competitive and stratified school, boys are saturated with convergent reasoning. They assume that this and the ability to get good examination marks are one and the same; and the more successful they are, the more perceptive about each other's powers of convergent reasoning they become. Conversely, the more successful they are, the less sensitive they are to each other's capacity to diverge.

The Perception of Character

The next piece of work under the general heading of self-perception concerns convergers' and divergers' perceptions of their own social behaviour and inner workings. Some readers of *Contrary Imaginations* concluded, not entirely unreasonably, that convergers and divergers were none other than introverts and extraverts[25] – that time-honoured distinction now refurbished and transposed to an intellectual plane. They assumed that convergers were introverts, and divergers extraverts. This turns out not to be so. I have found the relationship between convergence and introversion as near to zero as a relationship can normally be expected to come.[26] Only three of the twenty-four items on the introversion scale of the *Maudsley Personality Inventory* produced anything approaching satisfactory discriminations between convergers and divergers.[27]

This result seemed a little surprising at the time, but has been

23. 3·3:1, P <0·005.
24. 2·5:1, P <0·025. Self-estimates of I Q and open-ended scores were relatively independent of the School List, the first being positively correlated to it, the second slightly negatively.
25. Eysenck (1957).
26. 1·05:1, n=75, range=fifteen to sixteen.
27. Convergers were more likely to answer 'No' to 'Do you like to play pranks upon others?' and to 'Are you inclined to take your work casually, that is as a matter of course?'; and 'Yes' to 'Would you rate yourself as a talkative individual?'

confirmed independently.[28] More rewarding were results from
the other scale in the *Maudsley Personality Inventory*: neuroticism. Divergent boys were more likely, overall, to admit to
neurotic symptoms than their convergent form-mates.[29] This
one might well have predicted on the strength of convergers'
greater defensiveness about emotional matters. In fact, though,
this correlation was achieved on the strength of only a few of the
items in the questionnaire. Eight items contributed solidly to
the discrimination; thirteen contributed little or nothing; and
three were actually tending to obscure it. Items positively
identifying divergers were:

*Do you have frequent ups and downs in mood, either with or
    without apparent cause ?* (2·1:1)
Are you inclined to be moody ? (1·9:1)
Do you ever feel 'just miserable' for no good reason at all ? (1·7:1)
*Are you frequently 'lost in thought' even when supposed to be
    taking part in a conversation ?* (1·6:1)
Are you often troubled about feelings of guilt ? (1·6:1)
Have you often felt listless and tired for no good reason ? (1·6:1)
Have you often lost sleep over your worries ? (1·5:1)
Do you often feel disgruntled ? (1·5:1)

The three positively identifying the convergers were:

*After a critical moment is over, do you usually think of something
    you should have done but failed to do ?* (1·8:1)
Are you touchy on various subjects ? (1·5:1)
*Do you have periods of such great restlessness that you cannot sit
    long in a chair ?* (1·2:1)

Clearly, there are conflicting trends at work within this
neuroticism scale. If it reflects emotional disturbance (and there
is evidence that it does), we can only conclude that neuroticism

28. In an unpublished study of Sussex University students, Ryle found no significant relation between scores on *Uses of Objects* and those on an introversion/
extraversion scale devised by Foulds and Caine (1965). See also Wallach and Kogan
(1965).

29. 2·3:1, P <0·05. Wallach and Kogan (1965) describe divergers as the more
anxious of the two.

in convergers and divergers tends to take rather different forms. The divergers seem more prone to feelings of depression and guilt; convergers to symptoms – *l'esprit d'escalier*, touchiness, extreme restlessness – denoting excessive emotional control. Other symptoms – obsessive qualities, for instance, and cyclic swings of mood – do not seem to discriminate consistently one way or the other. Both divergers and convergers are capable of owning up to neurotic symptoms; both are in all probability capable of being neurotic – each in their own fashion, the one depressive and the other over-controlled.[30]

Perhaps mistakenly, I have pursued the ideas of extraversion and neuroticism no further. There are clear signs, in fact, that the vein may well have more to yield. Sociability and emotional display are inherent in the notion of extraversion; and they are also components of the schoolboys' myth of the typical arts graduate. And the possibility of constructing new scales of neuroticism – separating out emotional defensiveness, depression and over-control – is not one that presents any major technical difficulty.

Myths, Abilities and Self

The last three chapters describe a web of relationships linking the mythology of arts and science to boys' choice of speciality, to their actual mental abilities, and to their self-perceptions. It would now be difficult, I think, to argue that myths and actual behaviour are unconnected. There are many questions to answer, even so.

For instance, the simplest question of all about myths: are they true? Granted that the arts specialist perceives himself as warm, and that he perceives himself as someone whom others see as warm; is he really so? Does he wear fashionable clothes, flirt with his secretary and panic in emergencies? And if he does

30. Some recent work on introversion and neuroticism has been based on a four-fold system of classification, Furneaux (1962). It might have been predicted that the majority of divergers would turn out to be 'neurotic extraverts', the majority of convergers 'stable introverts'. My sample does not support this. Divergers were, if anything, more likely to fall into the neurotic introvert quadrant than any other; the convergers to be stable extraverts.

all these things, does he do so only because we have told him that this is how the arts man behaves?

The evidence leaves this issue of causes open. We do not yet know to what extent the differences in perception described in Chapter 5, or in self-perception described here, antedate the choice of a career. If they do, a boys' tendency to halo the Novelist or Physicist, his clustering of adjectives, his responses to Actual, Perceived and Future Selves, could all be used to predict which way he will jump when a choice of career is thrust upon him. Conversely, such differences may still prove to be consequences of that choice rather than determinants of it. As far as mental abilities are concerned, the evidence indicates that individual differences are established before a career choice is made, and that the effect of a specialized training is to accentuate differences which already exist.[31] But it may be that biases in perception develop more gradually, and that they largely reflect boys' growing loyalty and commitment to one type of career as opposed to another.

Evidently there is a tangle here – of social pressures and psychological ones, of perceived and actual – and the unravelling has scarcely begun. Meanwhile, the ideas of self and self-perception seem worth pursuing; and in the chapters that follow, I propose to use them more assertively. Here self-perception has been used to embrace two distinguishable views of the individual. In a questionnaire such as the *Maudsley Personality Inventory* the individual is treated in minimum terms: as a passive reporter on his own behaviour. In the Four Selves he is ascribed more scope, and is invited to reflect on his own character and capabilities in more subtle and introspective terms. It is this second approach that I wish to elaborate: moving from what the individual says he does, to who he thinks he is; from the individual whom we see as a spectator, to the individual who sees himself as an agent.

31. Altemeyer (1966) suggests that a university training in physical science attracts convergers and appears to make them more convergent. The evidence on verbal/non-verbal bias of IQ, on the other hand, suggests little change between the thirteen-year-old level and university; Hudson (1960).

CHAPTER 7

SOME SIMPLE STUDIES

THE topic of self-perception is a vast one; as vast in a sense as philosophy and psychology combined. The experiments I now have left deal only with two of its corners. In this chapter, I want to consider the narrow area of divergent thinking, and to examine some subtle changes in the experimental situation which can transform the mental powers that boys display. These effects, sometimes quite dramatic, have a bearing on the concept of mental ability, and also less directly, I believe, on the relationship of ability to the perception of self. There are two of these studies, each carefully planned; and a third that was an accident. Together, they are the pivot on which much of my general argument turns.

Full Instructions

The first study concerns a small adjustment in the instructions of the *Uses of Objects* test, turning it from a test of divergence into one which is more convergent. The usual format of the test is completely open:

Below are five everyday objects. Think of as many different uses as you can for each.

The individual, in other words, is invited to write down whatever he sees fit, and has no clear restriction on subject-matter or time. When he is bored he stops. In the present case, these instructions were changed:

Write down ten uses for each of the three objects given below. For example, the following are ten of the uses that have been suggested for Elastic Band:
  1. *Using as a form of propulsion for a model aircraft.*
  2. *To hold trousers up.*

3. *To flick against an enemy's neck.*
4. *Stopping a flow of blood.*
5. *As a swing for an ant.*
6. *Melting and letting the hot liquid drip on someone's hand.*
7. *Putting round wrists to remind one of something.*
8. *As a catapult.*
9. *Burn to create a foul smell.*
10. *Attach to a snail, and see how far the snail can stretch it.*

Boys are given the target figure of ten responses for each object; and are shown by means of examples what kinds of response are legitimate. This modified version of *Uses of Objects* contained three objects rather than the usual five: Telegraph Pole, Jar of Treacle, Pane of Glass. It was given to a sample of boys who had previously completed a shortened version of the test in its open form, again comprising three objects: Light Bulb, Car Tyre, Pot of Jam. Although no time limit was announced under either condition, boys still writing after ten minutes were in each case asked to stop.[1]

Not surprisingly, perhaps, the impact of this change in instructions was substantial. Under normal conditions only 7 per cent of the sample produced 25 suggestions or more; with the more detailed instructions 65 per cent did so.[2] On the open condition, the three highest scorers produced 34, 33 and 29 suggestions respectively; with detailed instructions, and in the same space of time, over half the sample produced 29 or 30. A similar transformation was found in the quality of responses. Under the open condition, only 2 per cent of boys produced more than 18 suggestions which were unusual, witty, ingenious, or violent; with instructions, and suitably primed with examples, 67 per cent did so.[3]

It could be argued of course that as the two versions of the test

1. The sample consisted of 43 public school boys, aged fifteen. Experiments of this kind have often been done before – see e.g. Hyman (1964), and Datta (1963) – although not in the context of authoritarianism, nor of the contrast between convergers and divergers.
2. $3.8:1$, P <0.001.
3. Conversely, under the open condition 70 per cent of boys produced nine such responses or less; whereas with instructions only 4 per cent did so.

were given in the course of a single morning, the effect might be
due to practice rather than to the change in instructions. However, the evidence is against this. If there is a practice effect with
open-ended tests of this sort, it seems to be relatively small.[4] Nor
is there evidence that the three objects used in the second version
of the test (Light Bulb, Car Tyre, Pot of Jam) are any easier than
those used in the first (Telegraph Pole, Pane of Glass, Jar of
Treacle). In other words, the obvious interpretation seems to be
the correct one: that the sharp increase in fluency was caused by
the change in presentation. It follows that many boys can think
fluently if they are shown precisely enough what is expected of
them. The converger, in other words, is not so much the boy who
cannot think divergently, as the one who thinks fluently only
when told unambiguously to do so. ('So *that*'s what you want,'
they seem to be saying. 'Why didn't you say so in the first
place?') Of course, this is not to say that the divergent capacities
of all boys are identical. High scorers on the first condition still
tend to be the high scorers on the second.[5] Rather, it seems that
the fluency of most boys can be made to vary over quite a wide
range; and many have reserves of mental fluency that under
normal circumstances they keep to themselves.

At first sight, this may seem to destroy the fabric that I have
been at pains to construct. On reflection, I do not think that this
is so. What suffers is an old-fashioned framework within which
one still tends to envisage mental abilities: as attributes of the
human organism that can be abstracted from the context in which
they are exercised. In practice, it seems, the context is vitally
important. The convergent boys will diverge, but only when the
situation warrants it. And the nature of this warranty suggests
what it is that sets the converger at his ease: instructions. He
cannot proceed, especially into areas of emotional expression,
without clear and authoritative route signs.

This I feel sure, is part of what makes the converger a converger – and allows him occasionally to diverge. The full
explanation though is more complex. Clear instructions not only

4. See Appendix A.
5. For the quantity of responses, 2·4:1, P <0·025; for their quality, 10·0:1,
P <0·01.

allow the converger to plan his journey, they also shift the responsibility for travelling in the first place. Tending, as we know from Chapter 2, to be authoritarian and syllabus-bound, he feels that the blame for any unseemly emotional display will fall, not on his own shoulders, but on those of the adult who frames the instructions. That some such shifting of responsibility occurs, the second study confirms.

Playing Roles

The experiment just described deals with the obvious. This next one, although closely related, is altogether more fancy. It seemed possible that convergers might be more outspoken (and divergers even more outspoken than they already were) if they were encouraged to pretend that they were someone other than themselves. The experiment was conducted with a full version of *Uses of Objects* and a group of boys who had been tested in the normal way four months earlier. On the second occasion, boys were invited to do the test twice:

In this test, you are asked to perform two impersonations – to act two parts. First you are asked to pretend, for the next five or ten minutes, that you are Robert Higgins, a successful computer engineer. Higgins is a ‘boffin’ – a dedicated, conscientious man, with a logical mind and a gift with gadgets. Shy but friendly, he has two pet hates – woolly ideas and any show of personal emotion. Now, remembering that you are Robert Higgins, look at the five objects listed below. Your task is to write down as many different uses for each object as you can. Write down all the uses that you think would occur to Robert Higgins.

Now the second impersonation. Forget about Robert Higgins, and pretend instead that you are John McMice – the well-known artist. McMice is an uninhibited, rather bohemian figure. He often says things for effect, and likes to shock people with coarse or gruesome jokes. Remembering that you are John McMice, look at the same five objects listed below. Now write down all the uses that you think would occur to John McMice, however strange they may be.

As usual they were asked to put their names on their answer sheets; and as usual they were reassured that this was solely for the purpose of collation; and that nothing they wrote would find its way back in any identifiable form to the school staff. When testing I normally walk around the room a good deal; but on this occasion I kept my place at the front of the room and busied myself with piles of paper. There was no other adult present.[6]

Each boy completed the *Uses of Objects* test three times; once as himself, once as Higgins, once as McMice.[7] There was no doubt that boys were more fluent when playing the roles of Higgins and McMice than they were in their own right. Both the quantity and the diversity of their responses increased.[8] It was clear, too – as the test instructions invited – that the responses produced for McMice and Higgins conformed to the mythology of the typical artist and the typical scientist. Higgins's suggestions emphasized practicality and ingenuity; McMice's – as I shall illustrate in a moment – were more flamboyant. There was also a tendency for convergers to be relatively more fluent than divergers in impersonating Higgins, whilst the divergers were more at home in the role of McMice.[9] In the experiment on instructions, almost everyone benefited: the effect was to increase fluency all round. With Higgins and McMice, this was slightly less marked. High scorers under ordinary conditions tended to be high scorers four months later, but the association was not clear-cut.[10]

So far the results were not out of the ordinary. Their breath-taking feature was the enthusiasm with which some boys adopted the role of McMice. More than one seemingly respectable, upper-middle-class boy submitted an answer sheet, his

6. As far as I know, this experiment has not been tried before.

7. The five objects on the first testing were: Telegraph Pole, Pane of Glass, Pot of Jam, Shoe, Suitcase. On the second and third testing: Car Tyre, One Pound Note, Milk Bottle, Jar of Treacle, Elastic Band. There is no evidence that one set of objects is significantly easier than the other.

8. Responses for Higgins and McMice were pooled; although no credit, of course, was given for the same idea produced twice. The increase in quantity over the original conditions, $1 \cdot 8 : 1$, $P < 0 \cdot 001$, $n = 70$. Increase in responses involving wit, ingenuity, violence, or statistical unusualness, $2 \cdot 1 : 1$ $P < 0 \cdot 001$.

9. For quantity, $4 \cdot 0 : 1$, $P < 0 \cdot 01$; for quality, $3 \cdot 3 : 1$, $P < 0 \cdot 01$.

10. For quantity, $2 \cdot 1 : 1$, $P < 0 \cdot 1$; for quality, $3 \cdot 8 : 1$, $P < 0 \cdot 025$.

own name attached, bearing suggestions to make any respectable Freud-fearing psychologist blench. Some were obscene, others nauseating. One of the more jovial boys suggested that our Monarch be held upside down in Bond Street, and the jar of treacle poured slowly into what manuals of motherhood (but not he) would describe as her birth canal. This edited extract from his script gives some impression of his gusto:

HIGGINS (*Milk Bottle*) Holding milk, making bombs with, space capsule for a beetle.
(*Car Tyre*) Swimming in, running at high speed towards a wall in.
(*Jar of Treacle*) Oiling heavy bearings with so as to sabotage machinery, laying a trail for catching edible locusts in Australia.
(*Elastic Band*) Using as driving band for small motor.

MCMICE (*Milk Bottle*) Jamming penis in, storing baboon's testicles in for giving virility to impotent people, cutting throats with, symbol of Britain's middle and lower 'solid' classes, throwing at Edward Heath in motorboat.
(*One Pound Note*) Sticking on Op-art mural depicting magnificance of Britain, her Commonwealth & Empire, for burning slowly in front of a British audience composed largely of grocers, wrapping around a severed thumb, and pinning it on.
(*Car Tyre*) Playing giant deck-tennis with, putting baby in and leaving baby to grow up therein, until body can expand no further, try as it may ...

Another boy had the following to suggest for a milk bottle and a pound note:

MCMICE (*Milk Bottle*) Masturbate with it. Cut my mother's neck with a broken bit. Would have an interesting effect if broken up and shot in little bits at a nude. The milk would be good to drown someone in. Pump it up someone's nose, vagina. Could make pattern of interesting scars on a little boys arse.
(*One Pound Note*) Could buy hormone cream, contraceptives. Gives someone a burn on a huge pile of pound notes.

> Burn it in front of a beggar. Put up vagina, mouth, nose, and burn. Forge it. . . .

Some of his later inventions were too repulsive to read, let alone to print.

These seem a tribute either to the spirit of trust engendered, or to boys' innate foolhardiness. It is hard to believe that a roomful of fifteen-year-olds should reveal themselves so openly on so slender an excuse. The clumsy charade I arranged seems to have allowed them to dissociate themselves from their normal standards to an extent I had not guessed possible. Higgins and McMice were roles that seemed to come naturally; more naturally in many cases than the responses that boys had originally been willing to identify as their own. Especially with McMice, the performance often seemed less an impersonation than a release: as if a defensive barrier had been lifted, and a ready-made 'persona' within the individual given rare but spontaneous expression.

Between them these two studies make it clear that an individual's fluency is not a fixed feature of his mental life. It can be modified grossly by quite small adjustments of context. They also hint strongly that the fluency a boy displays is regulated by his sense of self. Before elaborating on so elusive a point, there is the third piece of evidence to describe – the one that was found by accident.

Some Fortuitous Evidence

One of the fictions of mental testing is the mental tester himself. Tacitly, he is assumed to enter the testing-room; introduce himself; establish what he is pleased to call 'rapport'; administer his tests; and depart – all according to unerring routine. On the occasion I now wish to describe, I slipped from this golden mean of equanimity. Testing a roomful of able fifth formers, my manner was more hectoring than in any session before or since.[11]

11. I was in a bad temper, and at the first sign of ill-discipline, raised my voice more than I meant to, demanding that the miscreant pull his wits together on my behalf. There followed an hour and a half of what every teacher will recognize: uneasy, slightly resentful calm.

It seemed likely that scores might be slightly depressed, reflecting the morning's mood. Yet in one respect, they turned out better than any I had seen, from that school or any other. The IQs were better than usual for such a group, although not significantly so; and likewise the scores on *Meanings of Words*. It was on *Uses of Objects* that the results were so unusual. Normally, the top ten per cent of boys in such a group produced 35 suggestions or more, and one or two sometimes reach the high 40s or low 50s. In the present instance over half the boys scored 35 or more, and the top five reached 87, 78, 77, 67 and 60 respectively.[12] What was true of the quantity of responses also held for their quality. The average number of witty, violent, ingenious or unusual responses in such a sample is rarely higher than 10 – a value exceeded in the present case by all but seven in a sample of 43. When compared with results from a carefully matched group at a neighbouring school, the difference was unmistakable.[13]

Perhaps the most surprising aspect of all was the improvement not only of high and average scorers but of low scorers as well. Normally the lowest 10 per cent of scores on *Uses of Objects* fall below 15. In the present case, the three lowest scores gained were 15, 15 and 16, with the next lowest at 23 – a score which would normally have placed its owners above the average for his group.

I have found no explanation of this unexpected excellence beyond the accident of my own evil mood. The boys seem to have had no special forewarning of the tests; and they were in no detectable way academically or socially exceptional. By dragooning them I seem to have exerted a pressure analogous in its effect to that of the clear instructions given in the first experiment. The spectacle of an angry adult may in itself have spurred the boys to try harder. It may also have helped to dissipate the air of uncertainty with which an open-ended task like *Uses of Objects* is surrounded: rather than dithering, unsure of what to write, they pitched in.

12. Presumably, the improvement was most marked in *Uses of Objects* because it is the only genuinely open-ended task of the three. I had met comparable scores only once, when *Uses of Objects* was set as part of the entrance examination to a Cambridge college; more of this in Chapter 8.

13. For quantity, 3·6:1, P <0·001; for quality, 2·3:1, P <0·001.

The Importance of Context

All three pieces of evidence mentioned in this chapter – the first two certainly, and at least arguably the third – hinge on the importance of instructions: their nature, or the way in which they are expressed. And instructions in their turn have a significance which harks back directly to the subject of Chapter 2, authoritarianism. The need for clear instructions is little more than the need for authoritative guidance; guidance which relieves the individual not only of uncertainty, but also of responsibility. And it seems that certain changes in instruction, in context, benefit almost everyone: to a greater or lesser extent nearly all of the boys in my experiments became more fluent.[14] Most convergers become less inhibited; most divergers less inhibited still.

The second study also has a wider and more speculative implication. It gives boys the licence to act out mythical roles that the tester sets before them. The fact that some convergers can don the mask of McMice and utter the conventional fantasies of artistic life suggests that they may incorporate, buried within them, selves – or scraps of selves, or persona, or personality systems, or response repertoires – that they normally suppress. And this possibility suggests, in its turn, that in choosing a career and a style of life, the individual is not solely concerned in acquiring certain skills at the expense of others, in picking up one slice of corporate folklore and ignoring the rest. Rather, he is involved in a choice among selves that already exist inside him. This idea is one that I expand on towards the end of Chapter 9.

14. A small minority were actually inhibited by the role-playing instructions, producing fewer responses than normal rather than more. Unfortunately, there were too few of them to detect any common characteristic.

CHAPTER 8

TWO PRACTICAL EXPERIMENTS

EACH of the three studies in the last chapter deals with the context within which a mental skill is exercised. The next two do the same; but the contexts now are broader and more diffuse. They deal not in instructions for mental tests, but with the impact of whole educational regimes. Already, a number of results have hinted at the importance of these; at the possibility that one type of regime may favour the converger, another the diverger: the 'sylbs' and 'sylfs' in Chapter 2, the differences between grammar and public school girls in their nomination of convergent or divergent form-mates, and the remarkable influence of a School List on boys' estimates of each other's mental powers.

In fact, Chapter 6 left little doubt that, at the fifteen-year-old level, a conventional English boarding school is a heavily convergent institution: an environment in which convergers are at ease and divergers wilt. On the other hand, it may well be that the higher up the educational ladder an individual climbs, the slacker this bias in favour of the converger becomes. The scholars of a Cambridge college, for example, are expected to show originality as well as excellence; and the same is sometimes claimed for candidates in Part II of the Cambridge Tripos. Even more is this true of the research student. He may not be original; but at least there is a statutory pressure upon him to seem so.

On this argument, one would expect university education to suit the diverger better than education at school. Is there any evidence that some styles of teaching suit the diverger, and others the converger? Or that divergers prosper more the longer they survive? One of my experiments approaches the first of the questions, the other the second.

Convergent and Divergent Teachers

First, a study designed to test the hypothesis that convergers learn best from teachers whom they see, and who see themselves, as convergers; while divergers are best suited by teachers whom they see, and who see themselves, as divergers. Experiments in teaching methods are notoriously recalcitrant. They usually demand a research design of great complexity; and even so, some snags are rarely overcome.[1] Still, the results are often worth retailing.

This particular study was conducted at a London teaching hospital, the in-coming medical students and their teachers serving as guinea-pigs. True to type, the method was complicated, and the results likewise. Both have been described in detail elsewhere and here I shall simply recount their gist.[2] Two successive years of students were studied, some 150 in all, plus the four members of staff who taught them. The course was a short one in elementary statistics.

Two of the four teachers tended naturally to favour the conventional didactic approach to their job, while the others taught in an exploratory fashion, and where possible used actual patients to illustrate the statistical points made. The first two were more retiring in manner and more impersonal; the second two more outgoing. One in each pair was an experienced teacher, and the other less experienced. Each was responsible for a quarter of the students in each year, and the design ensured that each taught convergers and divergers in equal numbers.

Before the course began the students were subjected to various measures of convergence and divergence: the usual IQ and open-ended tests; a self-assessment; a five-point rating made by their teachers; and a convergence/divergence questionnaire.[3] In turn, each of the four teachers was rated by his students, by himself, by his fellow teachers, and by me.[4] The amount of statistics

1. Those of artificiality and of what has come to be called the 'Hawthorne Effect'. See Young (1965). Experiments on the interaction of teachers' and pupils' personalities and cognitive styles are discussed by Torrance (1965); see also Cronbach (1967).
2. Joyce and Hudson (1968).
3. Joyce and Hudson, *op. cit.*
4. I sat at the back of some of the classes but made no contribution.

learnt was assessed by an examination, consisting of questions set in equal numbers by all four teachers.

Overall, there was solid agreement in the estimates of convergence and divergence, both for teachers and for students. Two teachers were seen as convergent; a third was generally agreed to be marginally divergent, and the fourth as unambiguously so.[5] The two experienced teachers, one convergent and the other divergent, also tended to get better marks for their students in the final examination.[6] The experienced convergent teacher was particularly successful with the convergers in his class; while the experienced divergent teacher did especially well with his divergers. This difference, though not large, was consistent from one year (and one sample) to the other. The inexperienced convergent teacher was also consistently more successful with convergent students. The odd man out was the relatively inexperienced and marginally divergent diverger. Contrary to expectation, he did better with convergers, worse with divergers; and he did so two years running.[7]

The results, in other words, are a little indigestible. Clearly 'convergence' and 'divergence' are qualities that both teachers and students can recognize in themselves and in each other. Clear, too, is the fact that the convergence or divergence of a particular teacher had a stable effect on the amount of learning the convergers and divergers in his class achieve. The oddity lies in the fact that the direction of this influence cannot always be predicted in advance: with three teachers out of four, like seemed to learn best from like; with the fourth, like learned best from unlike – two years in a row. The explanation is not easy to see, but may lie I think in this fourth teacher's personality. Despite a

5. Overall agreement of estimates, $4\cdot6\!:\!1$, $P < 0\cdot005$. Interestingly, the judgements made by the two divergent teachers and the students were in agreement. The two convergent teachers differed both from the students and among themselves.

6. $1\cdot9\!:\!1$, $P < 0\cdot05$.

7. The tendency for the convergent teacher to get better examination results for convergent than for divergent students (and the divergent teacher the reverse) was significant, as far as the two experienced, successful and clearly contrasted teachers were concerned; $P < 0\cdot025$. Over all four, it was not. On the other hand, the tendency of a given teacher's impact on convergent and divergent students to be stable from one year (and one sample) to another was highly significant; $P < 0\cdot005$.

friendly and informal method of teaching, he was judged only slightly more divergent than the two convergers, and as much less divergent than the other diverger. A research statistician by training, his slightly booming public manner seemed a disguise for shyness: a converger, perhaps, in diverger's clothing. It may be that the divergent teacher suits the divergent pupil only when his inventiveness and informality is matched by what his audience perceive as 'warmth'.

University Entrance

Now the second question: do divergers do better for themselves the higher up the academic system they go? The statistical evidence, albeit inadequate, suggests that they do. Among English fifteen-year-olds, as we already know from Chapter 6, the diverger is less academically successful than the converger in a ratio of more than two to one. At the level of university entrance, the balance has begun to redress itself. Of the fifteen-year-old convergers, divergers and all-rounders in my sample, nearly two hundred have now left school, and three-quarters of them have gone to university. The convergers and all-rounders were distinctly more likely than the divergers to reach university.[8] Of those admitted to Oxford and Cambridge, twenty-seven won scholarships or exhibitions; again, these were more likely to be convergers than divergers.[9] The convergers, in other words, still seem to be outstripping the divergers by the age of eighteen, but not as handsomely as they were three years earlier. Whether this swing towards the diverger will continue throughout university, it is at the moment too early to tell.[10] Few of my

8. Difference between convergers and divergers, 1·4:1, P <0·05, n=192. There were no significant differences in the percentages of convergers and divergers going to Oxford and Cambridge as opposed to other universities.

9. 1·7:1, P <0·05. All-rounders, like divergers, did slightly worse in the scholarship examinations than one would expect by chance. All but one of the convergers who won awards did so in 'convergent' subjects; mathematics, engineering, natural sciences, classics, economics. More surprising perhaps were two of the divergers, with awards in mathematics and classics.

10. Cropley (1967, 1968) reports evidence of just such a swing among students in Australia – even among those studying science. The evidence against any close connexion between IQ and success at university is now substantial: MacKinnon (1962),

convergers and divergers have yet graduated. However, the argument is carried a stage further in the second of the two practical experiments.

In 1963, a group of Cambridge colleges set an experimental entrance examination. This *Alternative Paper* was in effect an open-ended test in thin disguise, and was aimed to elicit imaginativeness rather than knowledge. It was designed for candidates whose academic background was relatively weak; but who might none the less show signs of a late-flowering academic talent, or some other intellectual interest or gift: leavening, in other words, for the collegiate dough.

The risks were considerable. The examination might well admit young men who turned out to be academically hopelessly inadequate; perhaps promising brilliance but never settling for long enough to express this in concrete form. In addition there was the difficulty of public relations. The fiction exists in Cambridge that places are awarded on the basis of merit; that only rarely will a student with a weak school record be given preference over one whose record is strong. And increasingly, especially over the last decade, the gap between fiction and reality has tended to narrow. Yet the *Alternative Paper* represented a clear break with this principle. Many of the candidates had relatively poor school records; and if their performance at university did not improve, they would be bound to get poor degrees.[11]

The *Alternative Paper* comprised five questions: one of these

Hudson (1964, 1966b), Gibson and Light (1967). This association seems stronger among American undergraduates than English ones (Eysenck 1947), perhaps because of greater reliance in America on multiple-choice examinations. In my own data, the association between I Q at the age of fifteen and academic success is 4·0:1 (see Chapter 6); that between I Q at fifteen and gaining university entrance is 1·6:1; and that between I Q at fifteen and eventual degree class is 1·5:1.

11. Undergraduates are here divided into three groups: scholars, exhibitioners and commoners. Scholars are normally expected to reach a high academic standard; commoners often do so, but this is not expected of them. The position of exhibitioners is somewhat intermediate. Scholars and exhibitioners are usually admitted by open examination. Commoners still enter by a variety of routes, not invariably academic. But even in the cases of famous athletes, the high born or the merely well-connected, certain minimum academic standards are usually imposed.

was *Uses of Objects*. In scoring this, both qualitative and quantitative considerations were taken into account.[12]

In all, 91 candidates sat the *Alternative Paper*, of whom 31 were admitted. These 31 covered a diversity of academic subjects, although the majority tended to lie towards the middle of the arts/science spectrum. A third took natural sciences, usually in biology or medicine; a further quarter took economics or law; 4 took engineering; 3 archaeology and anthropology; 3 architecture and fine arts; 2 history; and 1 moral sciences.

The vagaries of the Cambridge admissions system being what they are, it happened that not all the thirty-one candidates admitted had done well on the *Alternative Paper*, nor were all of those who had done well on the *Alternative Paper* admitted. From some points of view this may seem regrettable; from mine it was convenient. I was able to compare High and Low Scorers in terms of their subsequent academic achievements; a technical luxury which more rigorous examination procedures preclude. The *Alternative Paper* also had the virtue, experimentally speaking, of being genuinely competitive. The candidates sat it in earnest, knowing that their careers depended on what they wrote. It remained a simple matter to trace both High and Low Scorers through their undergraduate careers, to see whether my prognostications about them proved correct.

Of the candidates admitted, 10 were High Scorers on *Uses of Objects*,[13] Their results at the end of their first undergraduate year were disastrous. If, for convenience, we accept the rule-of-thumb that first and upper seconds in Tripos are 'good' degrees, whilst lower seconds and worse are 'bad' ones,[14] only 3 of the 10 High Scorers' classes were good. The percentage for Low Scorers – 25 per cent – was even lower; while that for the university as a whole is normally estimated to lie close to 40 per

12. A candidate was classified as a High Scorer if (a) his fluency score placed him in the top 10 per cent of the sample; or (b) if his fluency score fell in the top 30 per cent, and he also displayed clear evidence of wit, ingenuity or violence in the suggestions he made. All other candidates were classified as Low Scorers.

13. Eighteen were Low Scorers, and the remaining three failed to complete the test.

14. And that undivided seconds are split on a 50:50 basis between 'good' and 'bad'.

cent. One of the High Scorers who had gained a third left
the university altogether. On this basis, the young men from
the *Alternative Paper* were judged a very poor investment indeed.

By the end of the second year, there were perceptible signs of
improvement. The proportion of good degree classes among the
Low Scorers rose to 36 per cent; while 5 of the 9 remaining High
Scorers contrived upper seconds. By the end of their third year,
the High Scorers had improved again; while the Low Scorers
showed a slight relapse (33 per cent).[15] Of the High Scorers, 1
ended up with a first, 6 took upper seconds, and the other 2 lower
seconds. They showed, in other words, a clear improvement both
over their own first showing, and over the eventual performance
of the Low Scorers.[16] Their performance even rivalled that of
the university's scholars and exhibitioners. Proportions of good
degrees for scholars and exhibitioners in one college of the group
were 78 per cent and 63 per cent; the High Scorers (70 per cent)
thus actually outstripped the exhibitioners, and ran the scholars
quite close.[17] Moreover, the High Scorers on *Uses of Objects* took
good degrees in a variety of subjects – natural science (3),
archaeology and anthropology (2), history and law. And 2 of
them – beginning with thirds, taking lower seconds in their
second year, and ending with upper seconds – stayed on to do
postgraduate research.

Related Matters

Three other points about the *Alternative Paper* are worth mentioning: the correlation of *Uses of Objects* with another of the
questions set; the issue of social class; and the problem posed by

15. Percentages include those who left the university at the end of their first or
second year. Strictly, these figures represent the last degree class obtained.

16. $2 \cdot 3 : 1$, $P > 0 \cdot 1$, $n = 10$; and $2 \cdot 1 : 1$, $P < 0 \cdot 1$, $n = 28$, respectively. These probabilities are based on Fisher's Exact Probability Test; see Siegel (1956). Arguably, the
two-tailed version is more appropriate. In any case, the experiment ought to be
repeated on a more adequate sample.

17. Scholars, and exhibitioners, figures for 1964–7. Standards in this particular
college are among the university's highest; hence the comparison of High Scorers
with scholars and exhibitioners in other colleges is bound to be even more favourable
than the present percentages suggest.

candidates with very high scores indeed. Apart from *Uses of Objects*, the *Alternative Paper* incorporated a longer and more ingenious question set by another examiner, which required the individual to plan a journey to the South Seas. His materials were an elaborate airline timetable; some maps; and transcripts of travellers' tales. Also included in the question were a girl friend and broad hints of human sacrifice. Candidates who did well on *Uses of Objects* also tended to do well on the *Journey*;[18] and those who answered the *Journey* well were significantly more likely than others to get good degrees.[19]

Secondly, social class. Critics of the Cambridge admissions system often protest that it favours the upper-middle-class boy at the expense of those from grammar schools. Instead of rectifying such a bias, the *Alternative Paper* could well have made it worse. Unexpected questions like *Uses of Objects* and the *Journey* might flummox the unsophisticated, and play to just that brand of self-confidence that private education is supposed to engender. Fortunately, the statistical evidence does not support this. The baseline for such comparison is provided by the social composition of the university as a whole. In 1963–4, almost exactly half the candidates for undergraduate places at Cambridge were from independent, fee-paying schools. The proportion of successful candidates from such schools was a little lower.[20] Not more than half of the 10 High Scorers on *Uses of Objects* could be said to have come from privileged homes. Two went to fee-paying schools in this country; one obviously wealthy, came from abroad; two more, though products of the state system, were in fact from academic homes.[21] The evidence, in other words, is that *Uses of Objects* embodies much the same amount of class bias as the university's entrance policy as a whole. And what that is no one is as yet in a position to tell.

The third point, and an important one, concerns boys whose mental fluency is exceptional. It is often suggested that such

18. 4·2:1, P <0·001, n=91.
19. 2·1:1, P <0·05, n=31.
20. The actual proportions were 49·5 per cent and 44·9 per cent, Morrison (1964).
21. The proportion of students from fee-paying schools among Low Scorers was 50 per cent. Percentages were much the same for the *Journey*.

individuals are disturbed; that there is something wrong with them. The same may be said of those with exceptionally high IQs. The implication is that, for neurotic reasons, such people are channelling energies into thinking which ought to be absorbed elsewhere. I have no systematic evidence to offer, but I do have the impression that boys with exceptionally high open-ended scores tend to be socially disordered, while those with exceptionally high IQs tend to be 'schizoid' – that is, withdrawn or odd.[22] Unclear, however, is the sequence of cause and effect. One of the High Scorers in the Cambridge experiment illustrates the difficulty. He produced the highest scores ever seen on the *Uses of Objects*, and did exceptionally well too on the *Journey*. And it was he who took a third at the end of his first year, who involved himself in an elaborate scandal, and removed himself voluntarily from the university. Every indication was that he lacked application and self-control rather than talent.

Maybe there really was something wrong with this young man. Perhaps there was no ordered form of social life that could contain him. Equally tenable, on the other hand, is the view that he was disordered in a more relative and fashionable sense; that his personality just happened to be dissonant with the particular kind of order that a Cambridge college provides.[23] Granted these three elements – his divergence, his neuroticism, and his dissonance with his social setting – a variety of causal sequences all seem more or less equally likely. It is as plausible to argue that his divergence caused his dissonance, and his dissonance his neuroticism, as it is to argue the sequence in reverse – neuroticism, dissonance, divergence. As far as firm evidence is concerned, there are scant grounds for supporting one sequence at the expense of any other.[24]

22. Admittedly, the evidence in Chapter 6 from the *Maudsley Personality Inventory* lends only slight support to this.

23. Academic failure was otherwise restricted to Low Scorers. Happy to relate, the rich young man from abroad, although he began with a third, turned out to be one of the two 'sleepers'; improving each year, he ended with a hard-working upper second.

24. Similar cases among much younger children are reported by Wallach and Kogan (1965).

On the Other Hand

Reservations are now in order. These results are promising; nothing more. In the first place, the experiment was on a small scale. In most cases, numbers were so small that tests of significance were inapplicable. For this reason, if for no other, the experiment should be repeated. Secondly, it was parochial: it concerned Cambridge and its idiosyncrasies, not the university system as a whole. The type of undergraduate picked out by *Uses of Objects* and the *Journey* would not necessarily flourish say, at the Massachusetts Institute of Technology. The fact that three Cambridge colleges should instigate such an experiment is evidence enough that they are atypical: it also happens, even by Cambridge standards, that they have unusually high standards both in academic achievement and in tutorial care. The students whose intellectual potentialities they seem to have released might well have languished in a more impersonal setting.

There is also the question of academic speciality. High Scorers on *Uses of Objects* appear to have done well in subjects near the middle of the academic spectrum: in archaeology and anthropology, for example, and in medicine. There is no evidence here about academic subjects towards the spectral extremes: English literature, say, or physics. It may well be that qualities favouring survival in anthropology or medicine would prove lethal to the physical scientist.[25] On the evidence in hand, it would be a mistake to treat either *Uses of Objects* or the *Journey* as valid tests for university admission, even in the subjects of the intermediate range.

This conceded, the evidence remains heartening. It represents a modest success in an area where accurate prediction is notoriously hard-won. It also points a moral: the urgent need for not a single, uniform examination system, nor even for a variety of examinations of the same type, but for a variety of examinations of radically different types.[26]

25. On the other hand, Cropley's (1967) Australian evidence suggests the reverse: that even in the physical sciences, the divergent undergraduate may do well.

26. If a university is offering, say, 60 places in English literature, there is now every reason to admit these students by various routes rather than one: 10, for the sake of argument, on the basis of 'A' level results in English literature; 10 more on an

In the past such experiments have rarely been undertaken, for fear of academic disaster. The present evidence shows, I think, that the fruits of bureaucratic risk-taking are not invariably as sour as in prospect they may seem.

English examination set by the university; 10 because they have IQ scores above 115, and a strong confessed interest in literature; 10 on the results of an open-ended test; 10 because they have written some original poetry or prose; and 10 with a hat-pin. The 'pay-off' values of the six criteria can then be compared.

CHAPTER 9

IN RETROSPECT

EIGHT chapters ago, I held out the promise of a synthesis: a gathering together of the threads that the last seven chapters contain. The prospect now seems a little bleak, general ideas serving only too often as 'short cuts from one area of ignorance to another'. It is worth attempting even so, not because my studies have a strict, logical unity of purpose – they do not; but because they belong together, in the sense that they occupy the same field. I shall try to say what this field is; partly for clarity's sake, partly because my results suggest a new frame of reference for work on intellectual development as a whole.

Between them, the results of the preceding pages suggest a view of human development which stands midway between that of the psychologist and that of the social scientist – one now incarcerated, in fact, in the textbooks of social psychology.[1] It seems that we are bound to envisage the intellectual growth of the individual, the evolution of his characteristic frame of mind, as the product not only of his genetic endowment and hormonal secretions, but of a continual traffic with his context – with parents and teachers, examinations and curricula, prejudices and myths. And even when his frame of mind is firmly established, it seems that an individual's intellectual performance is partially conditioned by the audience for which, and the setting in which, it is produced. Hence transplantation from one context to another may radically alter the amount of mental ability he is free to display.

Faced with such a diversity of possible causes – genetic, physiological, psychological, educational, familial, cultural – I feel the need for a centre of focus; to feel that I am not merely working in a field, but with a particular crop in mind. Without this the evidence still sprawls. The idea round which my results have in fact coalesced is the familiar one of 'personal identity'.

1. E.g. Dewey and Humber (1966).

Much of what interests me most about 'the nature, functions and phenomena of the human mind',[2] relates in one way or another to our sense of who we are and the behaviour that befits us. And increasingly, I see our sense of identity as exerting a controlling influence over the intellectual choices we make, and the mental abilities we are willing to reveal.

Personal Identity

Usually called 'phenomenological', this emphasis on the individual's perception of himself and his own potentialities is in no sense new. It has played a central part in recent theorizing about personality and human relations;[3] and it has been used with specific reference to career choice.[4] On the other hand, it seems to have been assumed that because the idea of personal identity is associated with psychoanalysis and Continental philosophy,[5] it cannot be approached except by means of anecdote. Psychologists in the empirical tradition have fought shy. Yet I see no reason why Continental subject-matter and empirical method should not be united; why the individual's perception of himself should not be explored by means of mental tests, and related systematically to evidence about what he does.[6]

If queasiness about the events of the mental life can be stifled down, the alliance of phenomenological subject-matter and conventional testing techniques offers substantial attractions. It offers the prospect, in the first place, of more accurate, more parsimonious prediction. We make better sense of an individual's responses to his environment from the moment we discover what that environment and those responses signify to him. Secondly, it frees the experimenter from the rival hegemonies of

2. The *Oxford English Dictionary* defines psychology as 'The science of the nature, functions and phenomena of the human soul or mind'. As an Oxford undergraduate this seemed to me most inept; 'soul' I am still unsure of, but the rest sounds better and better with time.

3. Rogers (1947), Erikson (1963), Laing (1960, 1961, 1964), Jaques (1965).

4. Super *et al.* (1963).

5. See, for instance, Merleau-Ponty (1962).

6. Kelly's (1955) work on Repertory Grid Analysis was a valuable piece of pioneering in this direction.

billiard ball and putty. It provides him with a central vantage point, from which he can handle a wide diversity of evidence: the individual's mental capacities, his personality and interests – what he finds he can do, what he enjoys and what he fears; the conceptual oppositions with which his culture endows him; and the more concrete aspects of his academic environment – curricula, rival academic disciplines and teaching methods, and the conventions and rituals, for example, of laboratory life. And third, it opens up to the empirically-minded just those areas of human action where more conventional methods of measurement have disappointed us most: the success or failure of the individual's adaptation to his career; the processes of intellectual discovery;[7] and the bearing of someone's working life on his private one – in particular to those relations that exist in and around matrimony.[8]

In the present case, there is also a fourth and more specific advantage. The application of empirical methods to the study of identity may unify various styles of research now scattered for lack of a central, schematic core. Take the parallelism between the values underlying myths of the arts and sciences and the dimensions discussed in Chapters 2 and 3. It may be that a single system of values embraces the individual's perceptions of academic institutions; his perception of himself; and his demonstrable behaviour. That the oppositions between authority and freedom, self-expression and self-control, and masculinity and femininity are among the basic conflicts around which an individual's mental life develops, and that they colour his responses to a wide range of logically unrelated issues. These oppositions may be 'basic', not for arbitrary statistical reasons nor for explanatory convenience, but because they represent some of the earliest developmental crises through which each individual in this particular culture passes: the impact of parental authority; the demand for self-control, first physical and later verbal; and the establishment of a satisfactory sexual identity. This possibility of a synthesis incorporating work on intellectual abilities and interests, on perception both of self and of context, and on

7. MacKinnon (1963).
8. Laing *et al.* (1966), Mishler and Waxler (1965).

the upbringing and developmental crises of small children seems distinctly invigorating.[9]

Of course, no method is without its drawbacks and the phenomenological approach has several.[10] My feeling, however, is that reluctance to do empirical work on self-perception is ideological, and stems not so much from genuine difficulties, as from a more superstitious fear of the mentalistic. This I take to be a remnant of extreme behaviourism, and the 'quaint honour' that the psychologist should consider nothing but what he can see.

Difficulties notwithstanding, I accept Erikson's view that a characteristic concern of adolescence is the fashioning of an identity, a way of life that is habitable. This is a period when '... each youth must forge for himself some central perspective and direction, some working unity, out of the effective remnants of his childhood ... he must detect some meaningful resemblance between what he has come to see in himself and what his sharpened awareness tells him others judge and expect him to be ...'[11]

And I would add – as a working hypothesis – that once fashioned, this sense of identity serves as a self-regulating device, controlling the amount of ourselves that we permit to show. More specifically, that it is the 'fit' or congruence between our sense of identity and our perception of any particular context that limits what ability and what feelings we are able on that occasion to display. And more specifically still, that our perception of both self and context is framed in terms of a few

9. There are echoes here of the schemata in Bartlett's (1932) studies of memory; also, I think, of the structural anthropology of Lévi-Strauss. Lévi-Strauss has used the myths and rituals of primitive peoples to illuminate the 'structure of the mind' – the systems of mental association and opposition that shape both the culture man creates and his perception of it once created. My interest lies, however, in the individual's capacity for choice – his freedom to select one aspect of a myth rather than another in establishing his personal identity, and in the relation of these choices to the abilities and temperamental qualities he shows. For an introduction to Lévi-Strauss, see Leach (1967).

10. There are many respects in which objective considerations constrain the individual absolutely. Whatever his self-perceptions, a microcephalic child can at present have no hope of growing up to win a Nobel Prize. More generally, genetic factors set limits to the abilities an individual can hope to produce; Erlenmeyer-Kimling and Jarvik (1963). Conversely, superb levels of skill are sometimes achieved without insight or reflection – *idiots savants* are a case in point.

11. Erikson (1962), p. 14.

basic dimensions – of which respect for authority, convergence/divergence and sexual identification (or dimensions closely allied to these) are three.[12]

I now envisage the choice between arts and sciences as one of the first of the major steps that the able adolescent takes towards his adult identity. This is often the individual's first opportunity to select and reject from among the ways of life that his culture offers; his first attempt to fit a chosen style of thinking into some semblance of harmony with his more private needs. To make sense of this process, one must take into account not just the reality of the social options before the individual, but – as Carl Rogers has urged – his 'reality-as-perceived'. In attempting to analyse an individual's way of life, one cannot think solely, or even primarily, in terms of examinations and jobs, salaries and pension schemes; rather of the conceptual framework within which his idea of himself, his past and his future are conceived.

Future Possibilities

The emphasis placed here on the monitoring functions of human self-perception has connexions with a number of other more sociological ideas about the channelling of human talent – not only with the concepts of myth and role as they are used here, but those of reference groups, and of anticipatory socialization.[13] It might be of interest, on some other occasion, to work these connexions out in detail.

Whether or not such general formulations are felt to be helpful seems largely a matter of taste. Certainly, specific lines of research are now open. Work on the mythology of occupations and professions can be elaborated, not only to reveal more of their

12. The phenomenological approach can be pushed to extreme, but to do so is, I think, a mistake. It might be argued, for instance, that the 'objective' features of ability, temperament and context only signify in as much as the individual perceives them; that behaviour flows exclusively neither from self nor context, but from the individual's perception of the interaction between them. My view, however, is the conventional one: that although our self-awareness is our most sophisticated regulative property, its relevance is largely restricted to the more complex and subtle aspects of our behaviour. Most simple skills we perform automatically; and even in the performance of more complex ones, we frequently appear driven willy-nilly.

13. Jones and Gerard (1967); Musgrave (1967); also Butler (1968), who offers a useful review.

origins and influence, but also their bearing on groups that border each other closely: the theoretical as opposed to the experimental physicist; the physicist and the chemist; the experimental psychologist and the personality theorist.[14] There are technical possibilities too: the halo effect and the clustering of adjectives could be set to work as measures of identification or loyalty; and the *Four Selves* as a measure of the impact on the individual of various styles of teaching or of school regime.

The present results also suggest a broadening scope. There is a need for studies of much younger children: of the embryonic converger and diverger, and the relation of scientific and aesthetic interests to sexual maturity and to the 'sharpening' of stereotyped perception. At present, too, we know almost nothing about the development of differences in children's perceptions of themselves.[15]

If we look at children, we are bound to look at parents; at the homes that produce convergers and those that produce divergers – and at convergers and divergers who are themselves parents. Again, we are largely ignorant about the ways in which differences in intellectual type reflect themselves in the personal lives of the individuals concerned.[16]

Authority and its effect on intellectual development is a topic as yet no more than broached. Sorely needed are studies, not only of 'sylbs' and 'sylfs', but ones that take a realistic view of the function of fear in students' minds – fear of authority, of punishment and of failure.[17] We need to know how the various

14. There are signs that social class and fantasies of social class have more relevance to these myths than Chapters 4 and 5 suggest. The distinction in science between 'applied' and 'pure', and the hierarchy of prestige from social and biological science to physical science may be transpositions of the social class distinction between artisan and gentleman. Medawar (1967).

15. It would be interesting to know whether future scientists and engineers are more likely than other small children to view their own bodies in mechanical terms; whether future biologists, as Roe's (1953) evidence suggests, are preoccupied with disease and bodily decay.

16. There is evidence that physical science specialists show little interest in girls in adolescence, but marry younger than other students, Schroder (1963); also Roe (1953). It seems that convergers may tend to lightning romance and happy, uneventful marriage; divergers to relationships that are more confused. If so, this has a bearing on the 'rival systems of defence' postulated in *Contrary Imaginations*, Chapter 5.

17. Henry (1963), Holt (1964), Laing (1967).

systems of academic and social control used in schools and
universities influence their occupants' perceptions of themselves, of each other, of the system itself, and of what they learn.
Whether, for example, as studies of initiation ceremonies suggest, a ferocious regime raises the self-esteem of those who survive it; whether, conversely, what is painlessly won is poorly
regarded.[18]

It is a commonplace that the face of science can now transform
itself within a decade; less familiar are recent changes in the
patterns of recruitment to it. Against every economic of educational prediction, the proportion of able young men and women
entering physical science subjects at English universities has
begun to decline.[19] Counterbalancing this swing from physical
science – in this country at least – is one towards such subjects as
psychology and sociology. And correlated with it are a number of
others: an increase in the affluence of young people; a relaxation
in censorship and public prudery; an increased concern among
students for self-determination; changes in the pattern of
specialization in schools; the slow but steady drop in the age of
sexual maturity; the relaxation of clearly defined sex roles – for
instance, in matters of dress; and an increase in the rates of
illegitimacy and juvenile delinquency. There is no obvious
explanation of these changes: the problem is a set-piece, in other
words, for interdisciplinary research.[20]

Each of these suggestions concerns factual information; and if
it concerns theory, it does so only within a narrow range.[21] A

18. Aronson and Mills (1959). Also Lawrence and Festinger (1962), and the discussion in Jones and Gerard (1967).
19. Dainton (1968), Butler (1968). Figures suggest that this 'Swing from Science'
is much less marked in Scotland than in England and Wales; that it is marked in
West Germany, the Netherlands and Australia; but absent in France, and also, it
seems, in the United States.
20. It would be of interest to know whether the distinction reported in Chapter 4
between the 'attractiveness' and 'social value' of the physical scientist is as marked in
Scottish schools as it is in English ones. Also whether methods of teaching designed –
in the words of the Dainton Report's third recommendation – to 'infuse breadth,
humanity, and up-to-dateness into the science curriculum' do in fact have a beneficial
influence on recruitment.
21. There are also biological possibilities. In the next few years we will doubt-
less learn more about the influence of sex hormones on complex human behaviour.
See, also, Zangwill's (1966) observation that although damage to the frontal and

more speculative line of inquiry involves the use of mental tests to elucidate the nature of personal identity itself. Both sociologists and psychoanalysts freely assume that there is more than one of us in each central nervous system: the sociologists that we are the sum of our various roles; the psychoanalysts that we take certain selves inside us and form an uneasy amalgam, using these as spare parts.[22] The theme is also recurrent in literature, and has a particular appeal to writers with sympathy for the theatre – Angus Wilson, for example:

She thought for a moment of going to see him in his dressing room, but then instead she gave the note marked 'immediate' to the stage door porter, for she had to hurry home to let Aunt Alice fall apart into all the various unrelated persons that she now knew bobbed up and sank down like corks in the ocean inside that old raddled body as inside all our bodies.[23]

On this argument, we have inside us a number of separate selves, some of which rarely see the light of day, and which counterbalance the self or selves we willingly profess. These appear like strangers at times of stress, or intoxication, or theatrically – or perhaps only when we dream, or in our sexual relations, or quite simply when we think we are alone.[24]

---

prefrontal lobes of the brain is known to have little effect on IQ, frontal lobe damage does seem to disrupt patients' capacity to think divergently. The suggestion is that convergence and divergence may implicate different cortical areas in the brain.

22. In Kleinian terms, 'part objects'. Of the psychological work on this topic, Laing's (1960, 1961, 1964) is obviously outstanding; of the more sociological, Goffman's (1959).

23. Wilson (1967), p. 382. 'She' is a novelist, Margaret Matthews, and 'Aunt Alice' one of her characters.

24. The significance of this last is brought home in a characteristically disquieting passage in John Barth's novel, *The End of the Road*. The narrator persuades a wife to snoop on her husband, a man of seemingly unwavering probity and self-possession. She protests that '... *real* people aren't any different when they're alone. No masks. What you see of them is authentic.' Reluctantly, she snoops all the same, and sees her husband – who thinks he is alone – pulling wild faces at himself in the mirror, doing military drill movements, cavorting. Finally: 'He turned slightly, and we could see: his tongue gripped purposefully between his lips at the side of his mouth, Joe was masturbating and picking his nose at the same time. I believe he also hummed a sprightly tune in rhythm with his work.' Barth's point is that it is Rennie, the wife, whom this invasion of privacy destroys. Barth (1967), p. 68.

Instances of multiple personality, of Jekyll and Hyde, can thus be seen less as mysterious freaks than as an extreme expression of a condition that embraces all of us in varying degrees.[25] And although superficially repugnant to the empiricist, this type of discussion can in fact be recast in behavioural terms. One can envisage alternative selves as alternative response repertoires, which – after the fashion of instinctive behaviour – are stored by the organism over long periods of time, yet can be performed fluently when elicited by the appropriate environmental cues. There is no reason why such repertoires should not be linked to one another in a logically complex way; nor for that matter why the repertoires, and the systems of self they represent, should not eventually be candidates for the experimentalist's highest accolade: simulation by computer.[26]

A formulation in terms of 'multiple selves' also offers us the chance to recast our conception of education in general and of career choice in particular. Instead of using, however covertly, the unseemly metaphor of pegs and holes, we can envisage the choice of a career as the endorsement, the fortification of certain among these possible selves or response repertoires at the expense of others. The influence of a professional training can be seen not merely as the imparting of certain skills and roles, but as the reinforcement of one among the many self-images that each student's head already contains. Little empirical work has yet been done on the changes of self-perception that occur in students whilst specializing; on the progress that Erikson describes, in which one's career gradually becomes part of who one really is; more generally, the consequences of apparently incongruous, even bizarre dissonance between public and private selves;[27] individual differences in the ease with which we slip from one self to another; the selves that we perceive as 'false', as

25. Thigpen and Cleckley (1957); Osgood and Luria (1954).
26. See, e.g. Newell, Shaw and Simon (1962). The weakness with behavioural reductions of this kind is their clumsiness. They tend to obscure the distinction between what a man does, and what he thinks he does; between what he could do and what he thinks he could do.
27. The woman who behaves like an animal in public, but in private is the perfect lady.

façade, and those we perceive as true; and the fascination, more generally still, of dissimulation.[28] It is the natural history of these processes that I should like to explore.

Convergers and Divergers in Retrospect

Before this chapter is finally abandoned, I have one last task; to take stock of the distinction between convergers and divergers with which I set out in 1962. Initially, I wielded this as a principle of classification; as a way of dividing schoolboys into groups. Only gradually have I become aware of its dynamic possibilities – and aware, come to that, of what the phrase 'dynamic possibilities' might mean. Yet even at the outset I was not pigeon-holing. No one was, or was ever expected to be, consistently convergent or consistently divergent. And although there is excellent evidence that people become set in their ways,[29] I have never seen why someone should not drift slowly over a period of years from divergence to convergence, or vice versa. Nor why someone should not be divergent in some moods and convergent in others. Nor why someone might not be convergent (or divergent) only when completing my tests. The converger and diverger are ideal types, in the sense that the extravert or the obsessive-compulsive are ideal. Such typologies function not as pigeon-holes but as reference points in terms of which the psychologist can map out the characteristics of an individual or group.[30]

Nevertheless, the character of my research has altered. In 1962 I was still subjecting boys to tests of the various psychological qualities and measuring their performance – much as I might have measured feet or femora. Gradually this has changed. I have become more interested in the experiential life of the individuals measured. Slowly I have grown aware, too, of the potential complexity of the relations between major psychological dimensions: that freedom in one area of a man's life may

28. Nabokov (1967) uses such phrases as 'games of intricate enchantment and deception' to embrace novel writing, chess and lepidoptery. The arts in general seem to depend not only on intuitive perception, but on illusion, legerdemain.

29. Bloom (1964).

30. Holt (1962).

counterbalance constraint in another. Also that convergence and divergence do not exist in a social or historical vacuum. More important, I have been slow to realize that the true function of ideas like convergence and divergence is to serve – like authoritarianism and masculinity – as signposts, indicating the essential principles or polarities on which the growth of intellect depends.

A grand taxonomy of human behaviour – an exhaustive classification – is, I am convinced, too vast, and too vastly boring, a goal to be worth pursuing. It follows that if categories like convergence and divergence are to earn their keep, they must do more than describe. They must be dynamic in the sense that they embody not merely differences but tensions. On this argument the individual who faces a career choice – one that he perceives as a choice between discipline and self-expression – does not merely slip towards one end of the spectrum of the possibilities open to him (to physics, say, rather than to literature); he is squeezed in that direction under pressure. The issue is central to his way of life. He is in the process of becoming the kind of man who finds security in intellectual precision, and fears an unruly sprawl.

It is in this sense that the distinction between convergers and divergers may prove of value. Such ideas may help to illuminate not the surface of human intellectual life, but the options, the tensions, that underlie it. They may help to unravel what is, after all, the central paradox of human development: that we may take two members of the same species and seemingly of the same culture, yet find that each finds satisfaction and peace of mind in precisely those intellectual operations that the other views with alarm and distaste. One, with Thomas Sprat and the founding members of the Royal Society, may see it as self-evident that 'the consideration of men and humane affairs may affect us with a thousand various disquiets', while it is the contemplation of nature 'that never separates us into mortal factions'. The other may flatly disagree. He may view Bunsen burners and dissecting boards with distaste, and assert, misrepresenting Pope, that the proper study of mankind is man.

The obvious weakness of my method, as of most others, is that it suggests a sense of order that the method itself may have imposed; that the parallelisms and clusters in my results may fragment when different methods and different assumptions are employed. Throughout this book I have adopted the fashionable premise that human beings think of themselves in terms of polar oppositions; and that the individual who ends up (say) as a 'plus one' converger does so as his own personal resolution of the competing attractions that extreme convergence and extreme divergence represent.[31] It is evident that I think in binary terms, and of tension between opposing values. This may prove a gross oversimplification.[32] The causes underlying our perception of the world may prove as amorphous and arbitary-seeming as the world itself. My hope of course is that there is enough in nature and the human mind that is polar to make my approach worth pursuing. If not, I can only throw up my hands – a binary beast – and leave the field to minds more subtle.

Happily, though, psychology is an activity in which the problems tower over those who attempt to resolve them. So although the probability of wasting one's time is high, certain knowledge that one is wrong is the exception. My prophylactic excursion into generalities over, I look forward to working again in more detail. A remark of Mary McCarthy's, about members of a utopia, reminds me repeatedly of the *intimacy* of much human action: 'No murderers or thieves applied, only ordinary people of ordinary B plus morality, people whose crimes that is, had been confined to an intimate circle, and who had never injured anybody but a close friend, a relation, a wife, a husband, themselves.'[33]

The vital moments in human development and their tell-tale signs, are not always, and perhaps not ever, well-advertised affairs, detectable with bold questions and simple-minded tests. They may be nothing more than subtle shifts in our feelings about the people around us and the ideas within us. It is with

31. See Osgood *et al.* (1957) and Kelly (1955); and on rather a different plane, Lévi-Strauss (1967).

32. Lloyd (1966), for instance, discusses polarity as a feature of early Greek reasoning.

33. McCarthy (1950), p. 14.

these seemingly slight details, redolent of who we think we are and what we would like to become, that the study of intellectual growth must eventually come to terms.

TECHNICALITIES

THE SAMPLES

No attempt was made to ensure that the schoolboys and girls taking my tests were a representative cross-section of English boyhood or girlhood. In several respects, in fact, they were atypical. All were above the national average in intelligence and academic ability, and the majority stood a good chance of reaching university should they wish to do so. Most fell within the top 5 per cent of their age-group, academically speaking; all, or almost all, within the top 15 per cent. The most brilliant among them were among the most brilliant of their age in the country. The sample was biased, too, both geographically and socially. With the exception of the students mentioned in Chapter 8, all were at schools in the South of England; and the large majority came from lower-middle, middle, or upper-middle-class homes. Relatively few were from the working class; and only one or two were more than vaguely aristocratic.

Except in the most exploratory of the studies, however, I did my best to establish a balance between the public and private sectors of the educational system. Unless stated explicitly in a footnote, each result was based on at least two (and sometimes four or five) independently collected samples. Sometimes, as in Chapters 2 and 3, samples from different schools produced inconsistent results. If there was no apparent reason for this – if, for example, they involved two schools of a similar character, and I could think of no other explanation – the result was reported as negative. If the schools in question did differ in some obvious way, I reported the difference and offered a tentative explanation. The research, on the other hand, was not designed with inter-school differences in mind; so where these occur, they should be viewed sceptically, and as little more than pointers towards further research.

THE DEFINITION OF CONVERGER
AND DIVERGER

The method used in classifying boys (and girls) as convergers, all-rounders, and divergers is the same as that in *Contrary Imaginations*. Scores on an IQ test (A.H.5) are placed in percentile grades: A to E – in the proportions 10:20:40:20:10. The same is done for each of two open-ended tests, *Meanings of Words* and *Uses of Objects*. Each individual's grades on these two open-ended tests are then averaged; and subtracted from his grade on IQ. Finally the resulting differential scores are graded again, and in the same proportions. As a result, 10 per cent of any given sample are classified as extreme convergers, 20 per cent as moderate convergers, 40 per cent as all-rounders, 20 per cent as moderate divergers, and 10 per cent as extreme divergers.

One weakness of this method is that it confounds two different creatures: the high-scoring all-rounder and the low-scoring one. A number of experimenters in this field have used a 2×2 classification, which distinguishes these – notably Wallach and Kogan (1965). I have tried a 9×9 system. Though cumbersome, these methods are without question more discriminative. If my primary aim had been to explore convergence and divergence in more detail, I would have adopted one or other of these more sensitive classifications. My chief interest lay, though, in relating convergence and divergence to the broader network of qualities – psychological, social, perceptual – in which they are embedded. Simplicity thus seemed in order; and doubly so, as my samples were already much more highly selected academically than any used in comparable studies in the United States. As a result, the kind of low-scoring all-rounder Wallach and Kogan report (the child who is academically apathetic and even mildly disorientated) crops up in my samples rarely if at all.

QUALITY VERSUS QUANTITY

Another criticism of the way in which convergers and divergers are defined points to the fact that this classification is based not on the quality of the individual's responses to *Meanings of Words and Uses of Objects*, but simply on their quantity. Sheer fluency and other qualities such as ingenuity, wit and violence demonstrably tend to go together; even so, there remains a case for including such qualities in the definition of convergence and divergence, rather than reporting them as correlates. The issue, then, is straightforward. Does the inclusion of such qualities as ingenuity, wit and violence into a single open-ended score change the classification of convergers and divergers enough to justify the vastly greater labour? The higher the correlation between the original method of scoring and a new composite one, the weaker the case for a change.

In practice, results are reassuring. If the total number of responses on *Uses of Objects* is compared with the total number of responses that are in any sense noteworthy (statistically unusual, witty, ingenious, messy, sexual, violent, obscene), the correlation is invariably high. For example, on a sample of 68 fifth form boys, $r = 0.75$; on a sample of 80 lower sixth form girls, $r = 0.86$. And when this sample of girls was retested four months later on a parallel version of *Uses of Objects*, r=0·83. In other words, individuals who are fluent but deadpan (like Fordham in *Contrary Imaginations*, p. 70) are the exception; and so too are those whose responses are few but telling.

CODING

The scoring of open-ended tests is sometimes thought to involve great difficulty, and large margins of error. With the simpler tests – *Uses of Objects* for example – this is only so if no adequate convention of scoring is established in advance. The process is laborious, but causes little more error than, say, the punching and sorting of responses to the *Semantic Differential*. Even here, of course, systematic error sometimes creeps in. Some coders have a taste for positive results, and their unconsciouses are not beyond creating them. Others grow hostile to the content of certain tests – a scientist's wife, for instance, asked to score *Semantic Differential* responses for Research Scientist's Wife – and their arithmetic suffers as a consequence.[1]

The analysis of projective material is a different matter. Our capacity to code in ways that support our own hypotheses is well known. One has to cope not only with the likes and dislikes of individual coders, but also with their resistance to the kinds of idea that projective tests elicit. In the coding of a standard set of stories, I have found the agreement between five independent coders to vary with the positions of those coders on the arts/science spectrum. Coders who are science graduates tend to disagree with coders who are arts graduates about whether or not a particular script is witty. Obviously, such analysis cannot lie in the hands of any one person, however overwhelming his probity.

The routine I have evolved is this. First, someone (usually myself) reads a set of scripts and outlines a coding frame, doing his best to foresee and forestall ambiguities of definition. The scripts and instructions then go in turn to at least two coders. They work independently, and 'blind' – knowing no details about the scripts' origins. I then collate the results, marking a script as possessing a particular quality only when both coders and I agree. I find from time to time that I have to refer back to the coders, to distinguish genuine differences in perception from conflicting interpretations of a vaguely worded coding instruction. If rival interpretations do exist, I reach a better definition, and return the offending scripts to both coders for

1. One cannot help wondering what atrocities the results of some sociological surveys must hide; and whether all the more faceless experimentalists are invariably as error-free as their own steely self-images imply.

another assessment on this particular point. The principle at every stage is that of omitting any script over which there is doubt. Not invariably as formal as I have made it sound, this procedure is far from foolproof. It does not guard adequately against coders who form their own hypotheses about how the various elements in the coding frame should relate, and pattern their coding accordingly. Nor against coders who share each other's prejudices and my own. But it does seem to avoid the worst excesses of unconscious bias.

STATISTICS

I have aimed for a uniformity of statistical treatment, so that results from widely differing sources can be compared directly. Quite apart from details of testing procedure and sampling, there are two separate facts that one needs to know about each discrimination or association reported: (i) its degree or strength, and (ii) its statistical significance – that is, its probability of arising by chance.

My data have sometimes been parametric, but more usually not – coming in rank order form, or in tables of 2×2, 5×3, 5×5, 7×2. The contingency coefficient is suitable as a measure of the degree of association for all these, but has certain trying disadvantages: e.g. that its upper limit varies with the number of cells in the table. For a 2×2 table, the upper limit is 0·707; for a 3×3, it is 0·816; and so on.[1] Easier to interpret, though on occasions wasteful of data, are the co-efficients used in numerical taxonomy, and appliable to 2×2 tables; in particular the simple matching coefficient.[3] I have used this in the analysis of adjectival clusters, reported in Chapter 5; but in general have stuck to my earlier practice of estimating the strength of an association or discrimination in terms of proportions of sorts to missorts – of cases that conform to a specified tendency as opposed to those that run against it. This and the simple matching coefficient are in fact closely related, but the proportion is the more readily intelligible of the two. Like the simple matching coefficient it is rough and ready, but gives a useful indication of how close a particular association happens to be.[4]

The only exceptions to this practice arose with certain results from the *Semantic Differential*, and with the correlations reported in this

2. Siegel (1956).
3. Sokal and Sneath (1963).
4. Though they may quote them to three places of decimals, psychologists often interpret correlation coefficients in simple verbal terms, as 'rather high' or 'rather low'. Even this is preferable to the widespread habit of misusing tests of significance (the X^2 Test for instance) as indices of association.

appendix. In the first case, some associations were so close that in terms of a 2×2 table, and of sorts and missorts, there were no missorts at all. Yet the associations were short of perfect. In these cases, I used Spearman's rank order coefficient (r_s); or if a measure of the significance of differences between correlations was needed, I fell back on the simple matching coefficient, and tested for significance with X^2. With data in this appendix, I have been concerned more with comparability with the mental testing literature, and hence have used Pearson's product moment correlation coefficient (r).

As a measure of significance, and whenever it was applicable, I used the X^2 Test, usually in its 2×2 form. Again, my main reason was uniformity. Much higher levels of significance could often be gained by using more sensitive tests: e.g. the Wilcoxon Matched-Pairs Test on test-retest data in Chapter 7. These were calculated for interest's sake, but the probabilities reported are from X^2. Occasionally, when samples were very small indeed, Fisher's Exact Probability Test was used, but in its 2-tailed, more conservative form. The only real difficulty experienced was in testing the significance of differences in certain 7×2 tables derived from the *Semantic Differential*. The X^2 Test gave some odd results, presumably because it treats each cell as discrete. In the event I used the Kolmogorov-Smirnov Two Sample Test, though on reflection the Mann-Whitney U Test might have been preferable. In general, the estimation of probabilities has erred consistently on the side of caution. Two-tailed tests have been used, except in rare and stated instances where a clear prediction was established in advance.

RELIABILITY

One of the canons of mental testing orthodoxy is that a test should give much the same measurements from one day to the next; that a boy classified as a converger on Monday should be classified by the same tests as a converger on Friday. This belief in 'reliability' has much to recommend it. On the other hand, it leads to absurdity if applied to open-ended tests without reflection. When compared with the test-retest reliability of an intelligence test like A.H.5, that of open-ended tests is decidedly low. When two parallel versions of *Uses of Objects* were given to the eighty schoolgirls just mentioned, with an interval of four months between testings, the correlation that resulted was $r = 0.53$. (Gross changes in score however, were relatively few; hence the proportion of sorts to missorts was higher than this value of r would lead one to expect – 11.0:1.)

Does this evidence of 'unreliability' demonstrate that we cannot place much faith in either of the scores that each individual produces? Certainly not. To conclude this we assume that first and second testings are mutually independent; that one does not influence the other – except perhaps to produce a small learning effect for all concerned. This is an assumption that we cannot make.

Consider the case of a projective test which requires the individual to tell a story. If we twice ask children to tell a story, and on the second occasion each child precisely replicates the story he offered first, we would assume, I believe, that we were all in the grip of some supernatural and malign force. In the story-telling situation, we expect – indeed we demand – variety of the child, and he expects it of himself. There are, then, two extremes: formal reasoning, in which we hope that children will perform like automata; and story-telling, where robot-like behaviour strikes us as peculiar, and where changes and fluctuations are the norm. We may hope that the boy who tells a good story the first time will tell an equally good one the second. But if on the second occasion, our invitation has lost some of its appeal, we should be interested rather than disappointed. And equally so if the reverse happens, and boys are more fluent on the second occasion than on the first. In general, we are prepared to find that story-telling is in some respects a 'one-off' affair.

A test like *Uses of Objects* clearly falls somewhere between these extremes. With open-ended tests of this sort, we expect a degree of consistency, but are not depressed if the agreement proves rather loose. Only bores, we bear in mind, tell the same story twice; only the deranged repeat the same violent idea time and again.

What on earth, the dyed-in-the-wool may demand, is the point of using tests which we actually expect to produce unrepeatable results? If the first testing is different from the second, and second from the third, which reading is the 'true' one? The answer should by now be clear: each is true after its fashion. If the first testing differentiates between variables of psychological or social interest – if it differentiates arts specialists from scientists, let us say – then it interests us; if it does not, it does not. Similarly with the second testing and the third. In terms of the canonical jargon, we justify the use of open-ended tests not in terms of their test-retest reliability, but of their external validity: their power to differentiate among variables other than themselves. Replication then falls back into place as the business of being able to reproduce such relationships, not on the same sample, but on one similar-seeming sample after another – to show that they are not flukes.

FAST AND SLOW STARTERS

Another of the technical checks often made on a mental test is that of 'split-halves', designed to measure its internal consistency. Wallach and Kogan (op. cit.) report high internal consistency for tasks like *Uses of Objects* – 'split-half' coefficients of the order of o·9, item-sum coefficients usually above o·8. I have not tried to replicate this, but have used the simplest form of the 'split-half' technique for rather a different purpose. The method is simple. Some medical students were set to complete *Meanings of Words* in the usual fashion, without a time limit. After they had been working for five minutes, they were asked to make a mark on the answer sheet, signifying how far they had gone, and then to continue as though nothing had happened. After ten minutes, they were stopped and moved on to the next test. The process was then repeated for *Uses of Objects*. The number of ideas produced during the first five minutes on each test was then compared with the number produced in the second five. My aim was to discover whether individuals' response rates declined steadily; fast at first but gradually petering out.

The result was unexpected. I predicted positive correlations between halves, only doubting how strong the correlations would prove. In fact, there was a significant negative correlation on *Meanings of Words*, and a zero correlation on *Uses of Objects*.[5] Although there was a general tendency on *Uses of Objects* for students to produce less in the second five minutes than in the first (in a proportion of 1·5:1), some who were producing the most responses in the first five minutes were producing the least in the second, and vice versa. Some were fast starters who dried up quickly; others only got into their stride after a considerable delay. One student produced 25 uses in the first five minutes and none at all in the second; two others produced 3 in the first five minutes and 24 in the second. Others were consistently fluent (31 in the first five, 20 in the second; 23 in the first, 15 in the second); others still were consistently inhibited (7 in the first, 3 in the second). This rather curious finding complicates the notion of the diverger as the man who pours out his ideas in a constant stream.

THE STATISTICAL COHERENCE OF CONVERGENCE AND DIVERGENCE

A troublesome feature of work on convergence and divergence has been the low correlations among open-ended tests. Sometimes these

5. $r = -0.40$, $P < 0.05$, $n = 72$; $r = +0.05$, $P > 0.1$, $n = 72$, respectively.

have been lower than those of each individual open-ended test with IQ. In *Contrary Imaginations* this was not so; but intercorrelations among both convergent and divergent measures were rather low. On these grounds – and despite the consistent differences observed between convergers and divergers – it has been argued that divergence cannot be a coherent human trait at all. [6] Wallach and Kogan seem to have laid this particular bogey, by allowing children to complete open-ended tests in a more relaxed, unhurried fashion. They find, as a result, discrete clusterings of convergent and divergent abilities. Similar clusterings emerged from the study of medical students discussed in Chapter 8; the results are perhaps worth mentioning, even though the issue is not, I am convinced, a particularly fruitful one.

A principal component analysis was performed on the tests given to the eighty medical students in Year 2 of the experiment. [7] The first component was highly loaded on four indices derived from the IQ test (Verbal, Numerical, Diagrammatic, and Total scores); and relatively slightly on four measures of divergence (Meanings, Uses, Con/Di Questionnaire, and Self-Rating). The second component's loadings were the reverse: high on the measures of divergence, low on measures of IQ. [8]

Though finding this evidence of statistical coherence mildly reassuring, I cannot help feeling that our concern with such clusterings is simplistic. Wallach and Kogan, though admirably sensitive to the possibility of interaction between their main experimental variables, do not seem fully to have realized that tests themselves may interact – not only over time, as in the test – retest situation, but within a single testing session. Individuals may let themselves go on one open-ended test and have no energy or inspiration left for others. Divergence may in any case be more specialized than convergence: the kind of person who can express himself fluently may also be the kind of person who is fussy about when he is fluent and when he is not. The converger may turn his powers willingly enough on to any suitably convergent task; the diverger may diverge only in areas of his own choosing.

On this argument one would predict exactly what Wallach and Kogan find: that the average intercorrelation among measures of convergence is distinctly higher than that among measures of divergence. One might go on to predict – boys being more wilful, girls more dutiful – that this difference in the clustering of convergent and divergent

6. See Wallach and Kogan (1965) for discussion of this.
7. Joyce and Huson (1968).
8. This degree of separation was itself highly significant: $P < 0.001$.

qualities would be more marked among boys than girls. This, again, is what Wallach and Kogan report.[9]

Granted that there may be such complex processes of interaction at work, I cannot for the life of me see why research in this field has placed so little confidence in demonstrable differences between convergers and divergers. If convergers and divergers differ, and in ways unconnected to the tests used in their definition, this is evidence that low intercorrelations among measures of divergence have been misconstrued. The correct tactic now, surely, is either to explore the inconsistencies of an individual's performance as a topic of interest in its own right; or to juggle with the various combinations and permutations of ability that both convergent and divergent tests yield, in order to maximize the discriminative power of these tests against some criterion other than themselves. The wrong tactic – doubly wrong because both defeatist and naïve – is to treat poor intercorrelations between indices as a knock-down argument against further exploration of the field.

THE DISCRIMINATION OF ARTS
FROM SCIENCE

Since 1957, the pattern of specialization in English schools has changed. When I first went testing, there were brilliant young men in my sample who had studied nothing but Latin and Greek with any seriousness since they were aged nine or ten; and many who had suffered not a day's science teaching in their lives. This has now gone. All the boys I now test are taught some kind of science until they are fifteen. The status of physical science in sixth forms has itself risen. And the clear definition of arts and science in the sixth form has begun to fade. One school which as recently as 1960 was offering only half a dozen combinations of subject in the sixth form, now boasts over 120. It has become fashionable there to take mixed courses, combining, say, mathematics with English; physics with Latin and Greek; economics with both history and mathematics.

Educationally speaking, this I feel sure is an advance; but from the point of view of research it has been a great nuisance. In the most recent work, samples of pure arts specialists – that is, boys taking history, English or modern languages – have dwindled almost to nonexistence. As a result, the category of 'arts specialist' has had to be

9. See their Table 16. Average intercorrelations among their ten measures of divergence were 0·34 for boys, 0·50 for girls. Equivalent figures for ten measures of convergence – 0·50 and 0·55 respectively.

bolstered up by including anyone taking two arts subjects, plus a third which is not scientific. Thus, the combination of history, English and economics has now had to be accepted as an 'arts' course, and so too has history, French and Latin. History, French and mathematics on the other hand, still is not. Samples of physical science specialists are likewise thin, but have not yet had to be diluted.

One last technical point is perhaps worth mentioning. Some hawk-eyed critics of *Contrary Imaginations* noted that the arts/science discrimination was achieved with an index of bias of ability on two types of test, rather than with absolute scores. Hence the possibility existed that the arts/science discrimination rested on one type of test alone, the other being a passenger.[10]

Is it possible that the arts/physical science discrimination achieved with Con/Di is no sharper than that achieved with IQ alone? The suggestion is easy enough to check, and proves to contain no more than a grain of truth; an interesting grain, even so. Taking a sample of 139 fifteen-year-old boys from three schools, one finds that the arts/physical science discrimination achieved by IQ alone is 2·7:1. That with open-ended scores alone is distinctly lower – 1·8:1; that with IQ and open-ended scores combined to give the Con/Di distinction, substantially higher – 4·0:1. In other words, IQ does contribute more to the discrimination than the open-ended scores, by about 50 per cent. On the other hand, neither contributes as much as both in combination. Moral: once again, it is the measure of bias that tells.

10. It has always been assumed incidentally, perhaps because methodological critics are convergent, that it was the open-ended tests that were the redundant ones, not IQ.

THE TESTS

A variety of tests are referred to in the preceding text. A number have been described elsewhere – Hudson (1966a), Joyce and Hudson (1968); and two are available from the usual test agencies (A.H.5 and the Maudsley Personality Inventory).

1. USES OF OBJECTS

This I have used in various guises. In its conventional open-ended form, with new and with alternative lists of objects; in a closed ended form, again with alternative objects; and as a basis for role-playing. All are described in Chapter 7.

2. MEANINGS OF WORDS

The form of this has not been altered, except that a new and shorter list of words was employed: *Bar, Eye, Post, Set, Stop*.

3. YIELDING

The rubric for this test is given in Chapter 2. The full list of questions and alternative answers is as follows, the order of alternatives being that used in the test's second, revised, form:

Which of the following seem to you the most suitable names for characters in a television play? Pick one from from each group of six.

1. The beautiful but foolish debutante:
Clarissa, Alicia, Anne, Hermione, Sybil, Patricia.

2. The portly and slightly dishonest business tycoon who would like his son to marry the debutante:
Bunton, Snyder, Robins, Ramsbottom, McCulloch, Jones.

3. The tycoon's ambitious, unscrupulous, girl friend:
Marilyn, Barbara, Wendy, Joan, Ethel, Margaret.

4. The blackmailer – the tycoon's girl friend's younger brother:
Monty, Rupert, Arthur, Sidney, John, Cedric.

5. The middle-aged detective who unmasks the blackmailer, and marries the debutante:
Marshall, McIlroy, Ames, Prufrock, Smith, Sneddon.

Consider the British Isles in the year AD 2000. What, in your opinion, is the most likely

6. Number of motor cars on the roads:
20,000,000: 15,000,000: 25,000,000: 10,000,000: 5,000,000: 1,000,000.

7. Average expectation of life:
75–79, 70–74, 80–84, 65–69, 60–64, 55–59.

8. Number of television sets:
30,000,000: 20,000,000: 40,000,000: 50,000,000: 70,000,000: 60,000,000.

9. *Average age at which people marry:*
20–21, 18–19, 16–17, 22–23, 24–25, 14–15.

10. *Total population:*
70,000,000:   80,000,000:   60,000,000:   100,000,000:   90,000,000:
50,000,000.

Which of the following places would you most like to visit on a holiday? Pick one from each group of six.

11. *Athens, Venice, Lisbon, Dublin, Edinburgh, Oslo.*

12. *Budapest, Vienna, Naples, Madrid, Paris, Berlin.*

13. *Mexico City, San Francisco, New Orleans, New York, Chicago, Boston.*

14. *Peking, Tokyo, Istanbul, Lhasa, Singapore, Calcutta.*

15. *Rio de Janeiro, Tahiti, Brasilia, Lima, Bermuda, Sidney.*

Of the following colours or combination of colours, which strike you as

16. *The most pleasant:*
Blue and Green, Blue and Yellow, Red and Yellow, Red and Orange, Blue and Brown, Red and Blue.

17. *The least pleasant:*
Yellow and Pink, Orange and Pink, Red and Green, Yellow and Blue, Orange and Yellow, Black and White.

18. *The most suitable colour for a sports car:*
White, Red, Green, Black, Brown, Blue.

19. *The most suitable colour for a family saloon car:*
Blue, Green, White, Black, Red, Brown.

20. *The most suitable colour for a young woman's dress:*
Pink, Blue, Red, Yellow, Grey, Fawn.

Which of the following forms of crime, vice or misbehaviour strikes you as the worst? Pick one from each group of six.

21. *Blackmail, Assault and Battery, Drunken Driving, Tax Evasion, Robbing Banks, Forgery.*

22. *Drug Peddling, Prostitution, Gambling, Striptease, Obscene Films, Obscene Books.*

23. *Neglect of Children, Financial Dishonesty, Unfaithfulness, Blasphemy, Cruelty to Animals, Drunkenness.*

24. *Cruelty, Disloyalty, Deceitfulness, Conceit, Greed, Cowardice.*

25. *Bullying, Stealing Money, Lying, Cheating in Exams, Telling Tales, Being a Bad Loser.*

Notes

1. This test seems to work well. Schoolboys find no difficulty in completing it; and hardly ever detect its true purpose.

2. Scoring is simplicity itself. The lower an individual's total score, the greater his 'yielding'.

3. An item analysis shows that Questions 22, 23, and 24 are unsatisfactory, in the sense that both graduates and schoolboys tend overwhelmingly to favour the same alternatives ('drug peddling', 'neglect of children', 'cruelty' respectively). These should be modified.

4. THE POEMS

The six pieces of verse used in this experiment were adapted from Terman (1930). The method depends on the presentation of a sequence of pieces of information. The first piece consists of the verses printed on an otherwise blank sheet of paper. This the individual retains throughout the experiment.

A   *Dreamily parting the silence,*
    Reaching up far to the sky,
    Under the slow-swaying pine tops,
    Floats the melodious sigh.
    All through the balm-laden fragrance,
    Harmony soaring on wings
    Bearing a strange incantation,
    Softly and sweetly it sings.

B   *Remember the man who in sorrow and danger,*
    When thy glory was set, and thy spirit was low,
    When thy hopes were o'erturned by the arms of the stranger,
    And thy banner displayed in the halls of the foe,
    Stood forth in the tempest of doubt and disaster,
    Unaided and single, the danger to brave,
    Asserted thy claims, and the rights of his master,
    Preserved thee to conquer, and saved thee to save.

C   *He is so still, so silently at rest*
    That, having come into his heritage
    Of lasting peace, he seems to ask no more.
    His eyes are closed. If he could open them
    Perhaps they would reveal celestial joy
    That is not meant for human sight to see,
    Such happiness as can be only earned
    By years of useful life and noble thoughts.

D   *When, to their airy hall, my Father's voice*
    Shall call my spirit, joyful in their choice;

> When, pois'd upon the gale, my form shall ride,
> Or, dark in mist, descend the mountain side;
> Oh, may my shade behold no sculptured urns,
> To mark the spot where earth to earth returns !
> No lengthened scroll, no praise-encumbered stone;
> My epitaph shall be my name alone:
> If that with honor fail to crown my clay,
> Oh ! may no other fame my deeds repay !
> That, only that, shall single out the spot;
> By that remembered, or with that forgot.

E   The place I'd like to be
> Is where the spreading tree
> Spreads its shade
> And is made
> By the gentle hand of God
> In the rich, black mud.
> And the brooklet ripples down
> To the other end of town,
> And the roses are in bloom,
> And the violets give perfume
> And the blue grass waves like bushes,
> And in the brook here wave rushes,
> – But instead – a dingy town !

F   How pleasant, as the sun declines, to view
> The spacious landscape change in form and hue !
> Here, vanish, as in mist, before a flood
> Of bright obscurity, hill, lawn, and wood;
> There, objects, by the searching beams betrayed,
> Come forth, and here retire in purple shade;
> Even the white stems of birch, the cottage white,
> Soften their glare before the mellow light . . .

These the individual is asked to rank in terms of (i) the appeal they make to him personally, and (ii) their literary merit. He records the rankings on a separate 'voting slip', which is then collected. In its place, he receives a second voting slip which also bears this additional piece of information:

The six pieces of poetry in front of you have already been judged by a panel of experts, each a person of outstanding literary knowledge and skill. They placed the pieces of poetry in the following order of merit:

Most literary merit	D
2nd	B
3rd	C
4th	F
5th	A
Least literary merit	E

Now reconsider these six pieces in the light of this extra knowledge and decide whether or not you would like to alter any of your opinions.

As soon as he has committed himself to two fresh rankings, this second slip is removed – and a third put in its place:

Three of the six pieces of poetry were in fact written by great poets, the other three by American schoolgirls:
  A *Schoolgirl*
  B *Thomas Babington Macaulay (1800–1859)*
  C *Schoolgirl*
  D *Lord Byron (1788–1824)*
  E *Schoolgirl*
  F *William Wordsworth (1770–1850)*

Again, he is asked to reconsider his judgements, both of personal preference and of literary merit. Finally a fourth slip, a fourth set of judgements, and the experiment is over:

The six pieces of poetry were all written when the authors were young. The ages are as follows;
  A *Schoolgirl Age 11*
  B *Macaulay Age 13*
  C *Schoolgirl Age 16*
  D *Lord Byron Age 15*
  E *Schoolgirl Age 5*
  F *Wordsworth Age 17*

Notes
  1. This cumbersome-seeming method works smoothly enough in practice. The test's obvious defect is its literary bias. Used with more varied subject-matter, and presented mechanically (either by projection on to a screen, or by one or other of the various teaching machine apparatuses) it might well prove a sensitive and versatile device.
  2. The analysis of change in this kind of sequential judgement is

laborious and confusing, especially if interaction between the judgements is taken into account, as well as differences between individuals. For this reason, the data are perhaps best handled by computer.

3. The 'full yield' position was assumed to be 'D, B, C, F, A, E', on the second voting slip, and 'D, B, F, C, A, E', on the third and fourth slips.

5. SYLLABUS-BOUND QUESTIONNAIRE

Below is a list of statements about schoolwork. Consider each item and place a tick in the appropriate column.

1. I like teachers who stick to the syllabus, and do not digress.
2. I put off written work until the last minute.
3. I keep my notes for each subject arranged in a logical order.
4. I find that I revise more thoroughly than most of my classmates.
5. I make a lot of careless mistakes in my work.
6. I take fewer notes than most of my classmates.
7. Interests out of school often make me neglect my work.
8. I find it difficult to concentrate on my work.
9. I do quite a lot of serious reading outside my school subjects.
10. I find schoolwork restricting and would like to have more choice in what I study.
11. I like to work at a precisely defined task.
12. Whether I like a subject or not, I do my best to get a good mark.
13. I often disagree with my teachers.
14. It matters a great deal to me that I should get good marks in examinations.
15. I do not spend much time on work outside the syllabus.
16. I would like more guidance in preparing for examinations.
17. I wish schoolwork was less trivial.
18. I like to have notes dictated by the teacher.
19. I think that my school marks are a fairly accurate reflection of my true ability.
20. I try to develop a genuine interest in every subject I take.
21. I tend to be erratic, sometimes working well, sometimes badly.
22. I find that I work hard when I am interested and slack when I am not.
23. Most schoolwork seems to me a waste of time.
24. I would rather pursue my own ideas than follow a syllabus.

Notes

1. Both schoolboys and undergraduates (Parlett, 1967) seem to

enjoy answering questions of this sort; they seem to see them as both relevant and unthreatening.

2. Item analysis reveals two clusterings. The first and much larger one contains questions dealing broadly with the syllabus-bound/syllabus-free dimension (1, 7, 10, 13, 17, 19, 21, 22, 24). The second concerns conscientiousness (2, 3, 6). Intercorrelations (in terms of sorts to missorts) in the first cluster range from 1·1:1 to 5·8:1, with an average of 2·5:1 (n=43). These figures compare favourably with those from items in the introversion/extraversion scale of the *Maudsley Personality Inventory*. (Equivalent figures were 1·1:1 to 3·7:1, and 2·0:1, n=50.)

3. An oddity, perhaps an important one, is the position of Question 21, at the centre of the first cluster. This question has the highest average intercorrelation with other items in the syllabus-bound/syllabus-free cluster, and yet ostensibly it refers to rather a separate quality. Erraticness of academic performances is, I suspect, one of the great unexplored topics of intellectual development (see Hudson, 1966a).

6. THE MAN AND BOY
(see illustrations on pages 138-9)

Boys' judgements about the Man and the Boy were on the 7-point scale normal for the *Semantic Differential*; Osgood *et al.* (1957). Man and Boy were rated separately, but on the same ten pairs of adjectives:

Confident/Frightened.
Soft/Hard.
Intelligent/Stupid.
Warm/Cold.
Clean/Dirty.
Dull/Exciting.
Worried/Unworried.
Strong/Weak.
Dangerous/Safe.
Friendly/Unfriendly.

They were also asked:

Now jot down your impression of what is going on in the picture, and what the people are saying. Try not to use more than 100 words.

Notes
1. The only difficulties encountered with the Man and the Boy

were those general to the coding of open-ended material. These are discussed briefly in Appendix A.

7. FEMININE ROLES

People disagree about how young men and young women should behave. Below is a list of activities and interests. For each say whether you feel

that it is suitable for young men only, for young women only, for both young men and young women, or for neither.

1. *Living alone.*
2. *Active interest in politics.*
3. *Carpentry.*
4. *Owning a sports car.*
5. *Swearing.*
6. *Visiting pubs alone.*

7. *Looking after someone who is ill.*
8. *Reading poetry.*
9. *Getting drunk.*
10. *Gossiping.*
11. *Mending clothes.*
12. *Being an intellectual.*
13. *Going to art school.*
14. *Hitch-hiking.*
15. *Interest in money matters.*
16. *Enjoying war films.*
17. *Telling dirty jokes.*
18. *Teaching in a primary school.*
19. *Being a lawyer.*
20. *Car repairs.*
21. *Mountaineering.*
22. *Smoking.*
23. *Cooking.*
24. *Being a physicist.*
25. *Looking after young children.*
26. *Discussing clothes.*
27. *Being a ballet dancer.*
28. *Watching wrestling on T.V.*
29. *Being a doctor.*
30. *Making a proposal of marriage.*

8. THE MAN AND WOMAN
(see illustrations on pages 141-2)

The format was exactly the same as that for the Man and Boy, except in the instructions for the second, open-ended half of the test:

Now sketch out the plot of a story – any story – in which either the man, or the woman, or both the man and the woman, play some part. Try not to use more than 100 words.

9. THE SEMANTIC DIFFERENTIAL

On this and the following page, you are asked to make judgements about types of people. There are no right answers – the judgements are entirely a matter of personal opinion. Your task is to rate each type of person on each pair of adjectives. For example, take the first person in the list below, the Mathematician, *and judge whether you think Mathematicians as a whole are intelligent or stupid. If you think of them as extremely intelligent, put*

a tick in the left-hand column under the heading INTELLIGENT + + +.
*If you think of them as extremely stupid, put a tick, in the right-hand
column under the heading* STUPID + + +. *If your feelings about
Mathematicians are not so clear-cut, place a tick somewhere in between:*

$$+ + + = extremely$$
$$+ + = very$$
$$+ = moderately$$
$$? = don't know$$

*Trust your first impressions and work quickly. Try not to spend more than
a moment or two thinking about any one person.*

30 Figures were used, in 3 sets of 10:

TYPICAL FIGURES

A   *Mathematicians.*
    Novelists.

Physicists.
Historians.
Biologists.
Barristers.
Artists.
Engineers.
Psychologists.
Athletes.

B Poets.
Good Fathers.
Army Officers.
Research Scientists.
Dukes.
Good Teachers.

    Good Mothers.
    Trade Unionists.
    Good Friends.
    Yourself.

C *Nurse.*
    Novelist's Wife.
    Research Scientist's Wife.
    Schoolmistress.
    Film Actress.
    Barrister's Wife.
    Clergyman's Wife.
    Engineer's Wife.
    Air Hostess.
    Doctor's Wife.

Ten pairs of adjectives were used for each set of figures. These were, respectively:

ADJECTIVES

A *Intelligent/Stupid.*
    Dull/Exciting.
    Valuable/Worthless.
    Feminine/Manly.
    Warm/Cold.
    Hard/Soft.
    Unimaginative/Imaginative.
    Lazy/Hard-Working.
    Rough/Smooth.
    Dependable/Undependable.

B *Intelligent/Stupid.*
    Dull/Exciting.
    Valuable/Worthless.
    Feminine/Manly.
    Warm/Cold.
    Hard/Soft.
    Unimaginative/Imaginative.
    Good-Looking/Plain.
    Rough/Smooth.
    Dependable/Undependable.

C *Intelligent/Stupid.*
    Dull/Exciting.

Hard/Soft.
Unimaginative/Imaginative.
Good-Looking/Plain.
Happy/Unhappy.
Feminine/Manly.
Warm/Cold.
Uncultured/Cultured.
Dependable/Undependable.

Notes

1. An extensive literature on this technique already exists, see Osgood *et al.* (1957). I have nothing to add, except to warn the unsuspecting that the test is exceptionally boring to do; and to some, infuriating.

10. TYPICAL GRADUATES QUESTIONNAIRE

Imagine that you are writing a television play about two boys who grow up as neighbours, and then go to school and university together. The first, a typical Arts graduate, studies English at university, and then goes into publishing: the second is a typical Scientist who goes on to do research. Both do well. They are now in their 30s, each with a wife and children – and they meet unexpectedly for the first time in ten years.

You want your characters to be as realistic as possible: and you have now to decide which qualities are appropriate to them. For example, if you think that – in real life – an Arts man is much more likely than a Scientist to be sociable, place a tick in the left-hand column. On the other hand, if you think that a Scientist is much more likely than an Arts man to be sociable place a tick in the right-hand column. If you are less sure that they differ in this respect, place your tick somewhere in between.

$$+ + = \textit{much more likely}$$
$$+ = \textit{rather more likely}$$
$$? = \textit{don't know}$$

IN SPARE TIME

Sociable.
Heavy smoker.
Heavy drinker.
Likes expensive restaurants.
Wears fashionable clothes.
Has fast car.
Keen on open-air life.

AT WORK

Works long hours.
Competitive with others.
Keen to make money.
Flirts with his secretary.

AT HOME – WITH CHILDREN

Affectionate.
Expresses anger.
Embarrassed (e.g. about sex).
Gives lots of presents.
Strict disciplinarian.

AT HOME – WITH WIFE

Affectionate.
Likes being alone together.
Faithful.
Shares money worries.
Discusses his work with her.
Finds her attractive.
Helps with household chores.
Likes her to look glamorous.

IN GENERAL

Gets into debt.
Prudish (e.g. about nudity).
Gambles.
Swears.
Gets divorced.
Panics in emergencies.

11. THE IDENTIKIT

You are asked to outline four characters – two married couples – for use in a television play. There are only three conditions:
(i) All four characters must be lifelike
(ii) They must be clearly distinguishable from each other
(iii) They must be constructed from the lists of qualities given below
The first list of qualities concerns the two men, Mr S and Mr T. Work down the list ascribing one quality in each pair to Mr S and the other to Mr T. Write down these qualities in the spaces provided on the separate sheet.

QUALITIES FOR THE TWO MEN, MR S AND MR T

1. *Enjoys close logical argument.*
   Dislikes close logical argument.

2. *Undependable.*
   Dependable.

3. *Manly.*
   Slightly feminine.

4. *Happier dealing with people than with things.*
   Happier dealing with things than with people.

5. *Interests are mechanical and technical.*
   Interests are literary and artistic.

6. *Sociable.*
   Unsociable.

7. *Enjoys talking about emotional, personal matters.*
   Dislikes talking about emotional, personal matters.

8. *Studied a science subject at university.*
   Studied an arts subject at university.

9. *Cold.*
   Warm.

10. *Imaginative.*
    Unimaginative.

The second list of qualities concerns the two women, Mrs S and Mrs T. Work down the list as before, writing your answers on the sheet provided.

QUALITIES FOR THE TWO WOMEN, MRS S AND MR T

1. *Dull.*
   Exciting.

2. *Wears fashionable clothes.*
   Wears dowdy clothes.

3. *Good looking.*
   Plain.

4. *Down to earth.*
   Romantic.

5. *Lively sense of humour.*
   Poor sense of humour.

6. *Inhibited.*
   Uninhibited.

7. *Comes from North of England.*
   Comes from South of England.

8. *Soft.*
   Hard.

9. *Has poor parents.*
   Has wealthy parents.

10. *Happily married.*
    Unhappily married.

Of the four characters you have portrayed, which most nearly resembles yourself?

Notes

1. This technique may well suffer from an ordering effect, the items that occur first in the list determining the clustering of those that follow. Some more random method of presenting the pairs is obviously desirable, but not easy to devise for groups.

2. The system of pairing attributes itself involves an artificiality that in future it might be as well to avoid. The same criticism applies of course to the *Semantic Differential*.

12. MR X AND MR Y

Below you will find two characters. Mr X who teaches physics and chemistry and Mr Y who teaches history and English literature. Write down the thoughts that you think might occur to each of them during a normal working day.

13. THE FOUR SELVES

The format, once again, is that of the *Semantic Differential*. The instructions ask for a more painstaking approach however:

On this and the following page, you are asked to make judgements about yourself. As you do so, distinguish as carefully as you can between:
(i) Yourself as you actually are (ACTUAL SELF)
(ii) Yourself as you would like to be (IDEAL SELF)
(iii) Yourself as your teachers see you (PERCEIVED SELF)
(iv) Yourself as you expect to be in, say, 10 years' time (FUTURE SELF)
Be as accurate and objective as you can, and avoid false modesty.

The 9 pairs of adjectives used were:

Intelligent/Stupid.
Warm/Cold.
Dull/Exciting.

Valuable/Worthless.
Feminine/Manly.
Hard/Soft.
Unimaginative/Imaginative.
Rough/Smooth.
Dependable/Undependable.

14. MR A AND MR B

Consider the two men described below, Mr A and Mr B

Mr A
Enjoys precise logical argument.
Dislikes the discussion of personal, emotional matters.
Has interests and hobbies which are practical or technical.
Is happier dealing with things than with people.

Mr B
Dislikes precise logical argument.
Enjoys the discussion of personal, emotional matters.
Has interests and hobbies which are literary or artistic.
Is happier dealing with people rather than things.

Their friends agree that these two men are quite different in character.
Both have their own strengths and weaknesses. Six of the adjectives given
below are ones which their friends apply to Mr A and the other six are the
ones which they apply to Mr B. Which adjectives are which? Record your
answers by writing A or B in the squares provided – in all, six As and
six Bs.

   Cold.
   Dependable.
   Exciting.
   Hard.
   Imaginative.
   Intelligent.
   Manly.
   Rough.
   Smooth.
   Soft.
   Undependable.
   Warm.
   Of these two men, one is an arts graduate and the other a physical
science graduate. Which is which? Of the two, which more closely
resembles yourself?

REFERENCES

ADORNO, T. W. *et al.* (1950). *The Authoritarian Personality*. New York: Harper & Row.

ALTEMEYER, R. (1966). 'Education in the Arts and Sciences: Divergent Paths'. Doctoral dissertation, Carnegie Institute of Technology. Cited in unpublished paper *Professional Education and Originality*, Leavitt, H. J. and Altemeyer, R.

ARONSON, E. and MILLS, J. (1959). 'The Effect of Severity of Initiation on Liking for a Group'. *Journal of Abnormal and Social Psychology*, 59, p. 177.

ASCH, S. E. (1955). 'Opinions and Social Pressure'. *Scientific American*, Nov. 1955.

BARRON, F. (1963). *Creativity and Psychological Health*. Princeton: Van Nostrand.

BARTH, J. (1967). *The End of the Road*. London: Penguin.

BARTLETT, F. C. (1932). *Remembering*. Cambridge: University Press.

BEARDSLEE, D. C. and O'DOWD, D. D. (1962). 'Students and the Occupational World'. In *The American College*, ed. Sanford, N. London: Wiley.

BLOOM, B. S. (1964). *Stability and Change in Human Characteristics*. New York: Wiley.

BLURTON JONES, N. G. (1967). 'An Ethological Study of some Aspects of Social Behaviour of Children in Nursery School'. In *Primate Ethology*, ed. Morris, D. London: Weidenfeld & Nicolson.

BROWN, R. (1965). *Social Psychology*. London: Collier-Macmillan.

BUTLER, J. R. (1968). *Occupational Choice*. London: H.M.S.O.

CARLSMITH, L. (1964). 'Effect of Early Father Absence on Scholastic Aptitude'. *Harvard Education Review*, 34, p. 3.

CORSINI, R. J. (1956). 'Understanding and Similarity in Marriage'. *Journal of Abnormal and Social Psychology*, 52, p. 327.

CRONBACH, L. J. (1967). 'How can Instruction be adapted to Individual Differences?' In *Learning and Individual Differences*, ed. Gagné, R. M. Columbus, Ohio: Merrill.

CROPLEY, A. J. (1967). 'Divergent Thinking and Science Specialists'. *Nature*, 215, p. 671.

CROPLEY, A. J. and FIELD, T. W. (1968). 'Intellectual Style and High School Science'. *Nature*, 217, p. 1211.

CRUTCHFIELD, R. S. (1962). 'Conformity and Creative Thinking'. In *Contemporary Approaches to Creative Thinking*, ed. Gruber, H. E., *et al.* New York: Atherton.

DAINTON, F. S. (1968). *Enquiry into the Flow of Candidates in Science and Technology into Higher Education.* London: H.M.S.O.

D'ANDRADE, R. G. (1967). 'Sex Differences and Cultural Institutions'. In *The Development of Sex Differences*, ed. Maccoby, E. E. London: Tavistock.

DATTA, L.-E. (1963). 'Test Instructions and Identification of Creative Scientific Talent'. *Psychology Report*, 13, p. 495.

DEGLER, C. N. (1964). 'Revolution without Ideology: the Changing Place of Women in America'. *Daedelus*, 93, p. 563.

DEVORE, I. (1965). *Primate Behavior.* New York: Holt, Rinehart & Winston.

DEWEY, R. and HUMBER, W. J. (1966). *An Introduction to Social Psychology.* London: Collier-Macmillan.

DORNBUSCH, S. M. (1967). 'Afterword'. In *The Development of Sex Differences*, ed. Maccoby, E. E. London: Tavistock.

ERIKSON, E. H. (1962). *Young Man Luther.* New York: Norton. Also London: Faber & Faber.

ERIKSON, E. H. (1963). *Childhood and Society.* New York: Norton. Also London: Penguin (1965).

ERLENMEYER-KIMLING, L. and JARVIK, L. F. (1963). 'Genetics and Intelligence: a Review'. *Science*, 142, p. 1477.

EYSENCK, H. J. (1947). 'Student Selection by Psychological Tests'. *British Journal of Educational Psychology*, 17, p. 20.

EYSENCK, H. J. (1957). *The Dynamics of Anxiety and Hysteria.* London: Routledge & Kegan Paul.

FOULDS, G. A. and CAINE, T. M. (1965). *Personality and Personal Illness.* London: Tavistock.

FRENKEL-BRUNSWIK, E. (with ADORNO, T. W. *et al.*) (1950). *The Authoritarian Personality.* New York: Harper & Row.

FURNEAUX, W. D. (1962). 'The Psychologist and the University.' *University Quarterly*, 17, p. 33.

GETZELS, J. W. and JACKSON, P. W. (1962). *Creativity and Intelligence.* New York: Wiley.

GIBSON, J. B. and LIGHT, P. (1967). 'Intelligence Among University Scientists'. *Nature*, 213, p. 441.

GOFFMAN, E. (1959). *The Presentation of Self in Everyday Life*. New York: Doubleday Anchor. Also London: ALPP (1969).

HAMBURG, D. A. and LUNDE, D. T. (1967). 'Sex Hormones in the Development of Sex Differences in Human Behavior'. In *The Development of Sex Differences*, ed. Maccoby, E. E. London: Tavistock.

HENRY, J. (1963). *Culture Against Man*. New York: Random House.

HIBBERT, C. (1967). *The Making of Charles Dickens*. London: Longmans.

HOLT, J. (1964). *How Children Fail*. London: Pitman. Also London: Penguin (1969).

HOLT, R. R. (1962). 'Individuality and Generalization in the Psychology of Personality'. *J. Pers.*, 30, p. 377.

HUDSON, L. (1960). 'A Differential Test of Arts/Science Aptitude'. *Nature*, 182, p. 413.

HUDSON, L. (1964). 'Future Open Scholars'. *Nature*, 202, p. 834.

HUDSON, L. (1966a). *Contrary Imaginations*. London: Methuen. Also London: Penguin (1968).

HUDSON, L. (1966b). 'Selection and the Problem of Conformity'. In *Genetic and Environmental Factors in Human Ability*, ed. Meade, J. E. and Parkes, A. S. Edinburgh: Oliver & Boyd.

HUDSON, L. (1967a). 'The Stereotypical Scientist'. *Nature*, 213, p. 228.

HUDSON, L. (1967b). 'Arts and Sciences: the Influence of Stereotypes on Language'. *Nature*, 214, p. 968.

HUTCHINGS, D. W. (1963). *Technology and the Sixth Form Boy*. Oxford: University Department of Education.

HYMAN, R. (1964). 'Creativity and the Prepared Mind'. In *Widening Horizons in Creativity*, ed. Taylor, C. W. New York: Wiley.

JAQUES, E. (1965). 'Death and the Mid-Life Crisis'. *International Journal of Psycho-Analysis*, 46, p. 502.

JOHNSON ABERCROMBIE, M. L. (1960). *The Anatomy of Judgement*. London: Hutchinson. Also London: Penguin (1969).

JONES, E. E. and GERARD, H. B. (1967). *Foundations of Social Psychology*. New York: Wiley.

JOYCE, C. R. B. and HUDSON, L. (1968). 'Student Style and Teacher Style'. *British Journal of Medical Education*, 2, p. 28.

KELLY, G. A. (1955). *The Psychology of Personal Constructs*. New York: Norton.

KLEIN, V. (1966). 'The Demand for Professional Womanpower'. *British Journal of Sociology*, 17, p. 183.

KOHLBERG, L. (1967). 'A Cognitive-Developmental Analysis of Children's Sex-Role Concepts and Attitudes'. In *The Development of Sex Differences*, ed. Maccoby, E. E. London: Tavistock.

KUHN, T. (1963). 'The Essential Tension: Tradition and Innovation in Scientific Research'. In *Scientific Creativity: its Recognition and Development*, ed. Taylor, C. W. and Barron, F. New York: Wiley.

LAING, R. D. (1960). *The Divided Self*. London: Tavistock. Also London: Penguin (1965).

LAING, R. D. (1961). *The Self and Others*. London: Tavistock.

LAING, R. D. and ESTERSON, A. (1964). *Sanity, Madness and the Family*. London: Tavistock. Also London: Penguin (1970).

LAING, R. D., PHILLIPSON, H. and LEE, A. R. (1966). *Interpersonal Perception*. London: Tavistock.

LAING, R. D. (1967). *The Politics of Experience*. London: Penguin.

LAMBERT, R. *et al.* (1968). *New Wine in Old Bottles*. London School of Economics, Occasional Papers in Social Administration. G. Bell & Sons, Ltd. (1969).

LAWRENCE, D. H. and FESTINGER, L. (1962). *Deterrents and Reinforcement*. London: Tavistock.

LEACH, E. R. (ed.) (1967). *The Structural Study of Myth and Totemism*. London: Tavistock.

LÉVI-STRAUSS, C. (1967). 'The Story of Asdiwal'. In *The Structural Study of Myth and Totemism*, ed. Leach, E. R. London: Tavistock.

LEWIN, K., LIPPITT, R. and WHITE, R. K. (1939). 'Patterns of Aggressive Behaviour in Experimentally Created Social Climates'. *Journal of Social Psychology*, 10, p. 271.

LLOYD, G. E. R. (1966). *Polarity and Analogy. Two Types of Argumentation in Early Greek Thought*. Cambridge: University Press.

LUNT, R. G. (1967). 'Specialization in the Schools'. In *Arts v. Science*. ed. Ross, A. S. C. London: Methuen.

MCCARTHY, M. (1950). *A Source of Embarrassment*. London: Heinemann.

MCCLELLAND, D. C. (1962). 'On the Psychodynamics of Creative Physical Scientists'. In *Contemporary Approaches to Creative Thinking*, ed. Gruber, H. E. *et al.* New York: Atherton.

MACCOBY, E. E. (ed.) (1967). *The Development of Sex Differences*. London: Tavistock.

MACKINNON, D. W. (1962). 'The Nature and Nurture of Creative Talent'. *American Psychologist*, 17, p. 484.

MACKINNON, D. W. (1963). 'Creativity and Images of Self'. In *The Study of Lives*, ed. White, R. W. New York: Prentice-Hall.

MEDAWAR, P. B. (1967). *The Art of the Soluble*. London: Methuen. Also London: Penguin (1969).

MERLEAU-PONTY, M. (1962). *Phenomenology of Perception*. Trans. Smith, C. London: Routledge & Kegan Paul.

MILGRAM, S. (1961). 'Nationality and Conformity'. *Scientific American*, 205, p. 45.

MILGRAM, S. (1965). 'Some Conditions of Obedience and Disobedience to Authority'. *Human Relations*, 18, p. 57.

MILTON, G. A. (1957). 'The Effects of Sex Role Identification upon Problem-Solving Skill'. *Journal of Abnormal and Social Psychology*, 55, p. 208.

MISHLER, E. G. and WAXLER, N. (1965). 'Family Interaction Processes and Schizophrenia: A Review of Current Theories'. *Merrill-Palmer Quarterly*, 11, p. 269.

MORRISON, J. S. (1964). 'Letter to the Editor'. *Cambridge Review*. 9 May.

MUSGRAVE, P. W. (1967). 'Family, School, Friends and Work: a Sociological Perspective'. *Educational Review*, 9, p. 175.

NABOKOV, V. (1967). *Speak, Memory*. London: Weidenfeld & Nicolson.

NELSEN, E. A. and MACCOBY, E. E. (1966). 'The Relationship between Social Development and Differential Abilities in the Scholastic Aptitude Test'. *Merrill-Palmer Quarterly*, 12, p. 269.

NEWELL, A., SHAW, J. C. and SIMON, H. A. (1962). 'The Processes of Creative Thinking'. In *Contemporary Approaches to Creative Thinking*, ed. Gruber, H. E. *et al*. New York: Atherton.

OSGOOD, C. E. and LURIA, Z. (1954). 'A Blind Analysis of a Case of Multiple Personality using the Semantic Differential'. *Journal of Abnormal and Social Psychology*, 49, p. 579.

OSGOOD, C. E., SUCI, G. J. and TANNENBAUM, P. H. (1957). *The Measurement of Meaning*. Illinois: University Press.

PARLETT, M. R. (1967). *Classroom and Beyond*. Research report. Education Research Center, Massachusetts Institute of Technology, Cambridge, Mass.

PARNELL, R. W. (1958). *Behaviour and Physique*. London: Arnold.

PARSONS, T. and SHILS, E. (1951). *Toward a General Theory of Action*. Harvard: University Press.

PRITCHETT, V. S. (1968). *A Cab at the Door*. London: Chatto & Windus.

ROE, A. (1953). 'A Psychological Study of Eminent Psychologists and Anthropologists and a Comparison with Biological and Physical Scientists'. *Psychological Monographs*, 67, No. 352.

ROGERS, C. R. (1947). 'Some Observations on the Organization of Personality'. *American Psychologist*, 2, p. 358.

ROSENBERG, M. (1965). *Society and the Adolescent Self-Image*. Princeton: University Press.

SCHRODER, R. (1963). 'Academic Achievement of the Male College Student'. *Marriage and Family Living*, 25, p. 420. Cited in *Marriage and Family Relations*, Williamson, R. C. (1966). New York: Wiley.

SEARS, R. R., RAU, L. and ALPERT, R. (1966). *Identification and Child Rearing*. London: Tavistock.

SELTZER, C. C. (1948). 'The Relationship between the Masculine Component and Personality'. In *Personality in Nature, Society and Culture*, ed. Kluckhohn, C. and Murray, H. A. New York: Knopf.

SIEGEL, S. (1956). *Nonparametric Statistics for the Behavioral Sciences*. New York: McGraw-Hill.

SNYDER, B. R. (1967). *Report on Massachusetts Institute of Technology Student Adaptation Study*. Education Research Center, Massachusetts Institute of Technology, Cambridge, Mass.

SOKAL, R. R. and SNEATH, P. H. A. (1963) *Principles of Numerical Taxonomy*. San Francisco: Freeman.

SPIRO, M. E. (1956). *Kibbutz: Venture in Utopia*. Harvard: University Press.

STEPHENS, W. N. (1963). *The Family in Cross-Cultural Perspective*. New York: Holt, Rinehart & Winston. Cited in D'Andrade, R. G. (1967), q.v.

SUPER, D. E. *et al*. (1963). *Career Development; Self-Concept Theory*. New York: College Entrance Examination Board.

TERMAN, L. M. (1930). *Genetic Studies of Genius*. Vol. III. Stanford: University Press.

THIGPEN, C. H. and CLECKLEY, H. A. (1957). *The Three Faces of Eve*. London: Secker & Warburg.

TORRANCE, E. P. (1965). *Rewarding Creative Behavior*. New Jersey: Prentice-Hall.

VERNON, P. E. (1965a). 'Ability Factors and Environmental Influences'. *American Psychologist*, 20, p. 723.

VERNON, P. E. (1965b). 'Environmental Handicaps and Intellectual Development'. *British Journal of Educational Psychology*, 35, p. 1.

VERNON, P. E. (1966). 'Educational and Intellectual Development among Canadian Indians and Eskimos'. *Educational Review*, 18, p. 79.

WALLACH, M. A. and KOGAN, N. (1965). *Modes of Thinking in Young Children*. New York: Holt, Rinehart & Winston.

WATSON, J. D. (1968). *The Double Helix*. London: Weidenfeld & Nicolson. Also London: Penguin (1970).

WHYTE, L. L. (1962). *The Unconscious before Freud*. London: Tavistock.

WILSON, A. (1967). *No Laughing Matter*. London: Secker & Warburg.

WINCH, R. F. (1962). *Identification and its Familial Determinants*. New York: Bobbs-Merrill.

WORSLEY, P. (1967). 'Groot Eylandt Totemism and *Le Totémisme aujourd'hui*. In *The Structural Study of Myth and Totemism*, ed. Leach, E. R. London: Tavistock.

YOUNG, M. (1965). *Innovation and Research in Education*. London: Routledge & Kegan Paul.

YOUNG, W. C., GOY, R. and PHOENIX, C. (1964). 'Hormones and Sexual Behaviour'. *Science*, 143, p. 212.

ZANGWILL, O. L. (1966). 'Psychological Deficits Associated with Frontal Lobe Lesions'. *International Journal of Neurology*, 5, p. 395.

THOMSON, G. P. (1964). *J. J. Thomson and the Cavendish Laboratory*. London: Nelson.

INDEX

INDEX